The Environment
OPPOSING VIEWPOINTS ©

William Dudley, *Book Editor*

Bonnie Szumski, *Editorial Director*
Scott Barbour, *Managing Editor*

OPPOSING
VIEWPOINTS®
SERIES

Greenhaven Press, Inc., San Diego, California

Cover photo: Digital Stock

Library of Congress Cataloging-in-Publication Data

Dudley, William, 1964–
   The Environment / William Dudley.
      p.   cm. — (Opposing viewpoints series)
   Includes bibliographical references and index.
   ISBN 0-7377-0653-8 (pbk. : alk. paper) —
   ISBN 0-7377-0654-6 (lib. bdg. : alk. paper)
   1. Environmental degradation—United States. 2. Human
ecology—United States. 3. Environmental policy—United
States. I. Title. II. Series.

GE150 .D83 2001
363.7'00973—dc21
                                                          00-050287
                                                          CIP

Greenhaven Press, Inc., P.O. Box 289009
San Diego, CA 92198-9009

"Congress shall make no law...abridging the freedom of speech, or of the press."

First Amendment to the U.S. Constitution

The basic foundation of our democracy is the First Amendment guarantee of freedom of expression. The Opposing Viewpoints Series is dedicated to the concept of this basic freedom and the idea that it is more important to practice it than to enshrine it.

Contents

Chapter 3: Is the American Lifestyle Bad for the Environment?

Chapter 4: What Principles and Values Should Guide American Environmental Policy?

Why Consider Opposing Viewpoints?

"The only way in which a human being can make some approach to knowing the whole of a subject is by hearing what can be said about it by persons of every variety of opinion and studying all modes in which it can be looked at by every character of mind. No wise man ever acquired his wisdom in any mode but this."

John Stuart Mill

In our media-intensive culture it is not difficult to find differing opinions. Thousands of newspapers and magazines and dozens of radio and television talk shows resound with differing points of view. The difficulty lies in deciding which opinion to agree with and which "experts" seem the most credible. The more inundated we become with differing opinions and claims, the more essential it is to hone critical reading and thinking skills to evaluate these ideas. Opposing Viewpoints books address this problem directly by presenting stimulating debates that can be used to enhance and teach these skills. The varied opinions contained in each book examine many different aspects of a single issue. While examining these conveniently edited opposing views, readers can develop critical thinking skills such as the ability to compare and contrast authors' credibility, facts, argumentation styles, use of persuasive techniques, and other stylistic tools. In short, the Opposing Viewpoints Series is an ideal way to attain the higher-level thinking and reading skills so essential in a culture of diverse and contradictory opinions.

In addition to providing a tool for critical thinking, Opposing Viewpoints books challenge readers to question their own strongly held opinions and assumptions. Most people form their opinions on the basis of upbringing, peer pressure, and personal, cultural, or professional bias. By reading carefully balanced opposing views, readers must directly confront new ideas as well as the opinions of those with whom they disagree. This is not to simplistically argue that everyone who reads opposing views will—or should—change his or her opinion. Instead, the series enhances readers' understanding of their own views by encouraging confrontation with opposing ideas. Careful examination of others' views can lead to the readers' understanding of the logical inconsistencies in their own opinions, perspective on why they hold an opinion, and the consideration of the possibility that their opinion requires further evaluation.

Evaluating Other Opinions

To ensure that this type of examination occurs, Opposing Viewpoints books present all types of opinions. Prominent spokespeople on different sides of each issue as well as well-known professionals from many disciplines challenge the reader. An additional goal of the series is to provide a forum for other, less known, or even unpopular viewpoints. The opinion of an ordinary person who has had to make the decision to cut off life support from a terminally ill relative, for example, may be just as valuable and provide just as much insight as a medical ethicist's professional opinion. The editors have two additional purposes in including these less known views. One, the editors encourage readers to respect others' opinions—even when not enhanced by professional credibility. It is only by reading or listening to and objectively evaluating others' ideas that one can determine whether they are worthy of consideration. Two, the inclusion of such viewpoints encourages the important critical thinking skill of objectively evaluating an author's credentials and bias. This evaluation will illuminate an author's reasons for taking a particular stance on an issue and will aid in readers' evaluation of the author's ideas.

It is our hope that these books will give readers a deeper understanding of the issues debated and an appreciation of the complexity of even seemingly simple issues when good and honest people disagree. This awareness is particularly important in a democratic society such as ours in which people enter into public debate to determine the common good. Those with whom one disagrees should not be regarded as enemies but rather as people whose views deserve careful examination and may shed light on one's own.

Thomas Jefferson once said that "difference of opinion leads to inquiry, and inquiry to truth." Jefferson, a broadly educated man, argued that "if a nation expects to be ignorant and free . . . it expects what never was and never will be." As individuals and as a nation, it is imperative that we consider the opinions of others and examine them with skill and discernment. The Opposing Viewpoints Series is intended to help readers achieve this goal.

Greenhaven Press anthologies primarily consist of previously published material taken from a variety of sources, including periodicals, books, scholarly journals, newspapers, government documents, and position papers from private and public organizations. These original sources are often edited for length and to ensure their accessibility for a young adult audience. The anthology editors also change the original titles of these works in order to clearly present the main thesis of each viewpoint and to explicitly indicate the opinion presented in the viewpoint. These alterations are made in consideration of both the reading and comprehension levels of a young adult audience. Every effort is made to ensure that Greenhaven Press accurately reflects the original intent of the authors included in this anthology.

Introduction

"Environmental problems are considered to be the social aspects of natural problems, and the natural aspects of social problems. The word environment, then, entails both natural and social dimensions."

—Jean-Guy Vaillancourt

The word environment at its most basic level simply means "surroundings." Sociologist Jean-Guy Vaillancourt of the University of Montreal notes that the word has in the past had at least two distinct meanings. Psychologists and other social scientists viewed the environment as the sum total of outside influences on the human individual, and studied how a person's "environment" affected his/her growth, development, and character. Biologists and natural scientists, on the other hand, used the word to signify the interaction of plants, animals, sunlight, air, and water that collectively make up "nature"—with nature being generally defined as excluding human creations and influences.

Beginning roughly in the 1960s, these two definitions of environment became more intertwined. Scientists and the general public became increasingly aware of how human activities were constantly affecting natural environments, and how these changes in turn were impacting the way humans live. One important factor in this developing consciousness was the 1962 publication of the book *Silent Spring* by Rachel Carson, who argued that chemical pesticides such as DDT threatened humanity, both by direct exposure and by the destruction of ecosystems. *Silent Spring* created an uproar. Writing of the public reaction to Carson's best-selling work, political scientist Robert Paehlke wrote: "Nature became more than something that existed at a distance from most of human settlement, and nonhuman species were suddenly not the only species at direct risk from human impositions on the natural world." Historian Linda J. Lear writes, "Carson was denounced by industry and government as an alarmist, but she had illustrated as no one else had before that humankind was part of the earth's ecosystem and that, by destroying a part of nature, all of life was placed at risk."

Carson's book is credited with sparking widespread growth of public awareness of the natural environment, culminating in the original Earth Day on April 22, 1970, when twenty million Americans participated in rallies and educational events. The speeches and other activities went beyond traditional conservationist concerns about national parks and wilderness preservation. Issues such as air and water pollution, resource scarcity, and overpopulation took center stage. The years immediately following Earth Day 1970 saw the birth or revitalization of numerous private organizations concerned with environmental preservation. In addition, numerous federal laws were passed and federal agencies created to prevent or mitigate human-caused degradation of the environment.

In the decades since the first Earth Day, much progress has been made in some of the areas of greatest concern: DDT has been banned, the most visible cases of air and water pollution in the United States have greatly improved, and global food production has kept up with human population growth. Still, new environmental concerns continue to be raised. Among these are global warming, the increasing rate of species extinction, deforestation, and the connection in developing countries between poverty and environmental degradation. The actions governments should take to protect the natural world—and the balancing of these concerns with economic growth and development—are a source of continual debate. How humans are changing the natural environment—and how they in turn are being affected—is one of the questions discussed in *The Environment: Opposing Viewpoints*. Environmental issues are examined in the following chapters: Is There an Environmental Crisis? How Can Pollution Best Be Prevented? Is the American Lifestyle Bad for the Environment? What Principles and Values Should Guide American Environmental Policy? The articles provide a broad spectrum of opinion on topics pertaining to the environment and the relationship between earth and its most dominant species.

CHAPTER 1

Is There an Environmental Crisis?

Chapter Preface

Easter Island, located in the Pacific Ocean, was settled by Polynesians approximately 1,500 years ago. They developed an agricultural society that supported an estimated population of seven thousand people. Their culture included technology that enabled the people to carve enormous stone statues on one side of the island and move them to the other side. However, by the time Europeans reached the island in the 1600s, only the statues remained. Archaeologists theorize that as the population expanded, deforestation and soil erosion caused a massive drop in food supplies, causing the Easter Islanders' civilization to collapse and disappear.

Lester Brown and Christopher Flavin of the Worldwatch Institute assert that humankind, by depleting such natural resources as clean air and water, runs the risk of replaying the Easter Island experience on a global scale.

> As an isolated territory that could not turn elsewhere for sustenance once its own resources ran out, Easter Island presents a particularly stark picture of what can happen when a human economy expands in the face of limited resources.... The human race as a whole has reached the kind of turning point that the Easter Islanders reached in the sixteenth century.

However, not everyone agrees that the global environmental situation is that threatening, and some blame Brown and Flavin and other environmentalists for attempting to scare the public with "gloom and doom" predictions. The late economist Julian Simon was a prominent advocate of the view that human ingenuity would enable humanity to find new resources or use existing resources more efficiently, and thus avoid the fate of the people of Easter Island. "Every single measure of material and environmental welfare in the United States," he asserted in a 1995 article,

> has improved rather than deteriorated. This is also true of the world taken as a whole. All the long-term trends point exactly the opposite direction from the projections of the doomsayers.

The viewpoints in this chapter express both cautionary and sanguine opinions on whether the global environment is in a state of crisis.

"Our planet's capacity is beginning to diminish, threatening our economic well-being and ultimately our survival."

The Global Environment Is Deteriorating

Eugene Linden

Eugene Linden is a contributing writer on science and technology for *Time* magazine and the author of *The Parrot's Lament* and other books. In the following viewpoint, he analyzes the preliminary results of a massive United Nations (U.N.) study on the world's ecosystems. Linden writes that the study, called Pilot Analysis of Global Ecosystems (PAGE), brought together 175 scientists from different countries and specialties. They concluded that the five major types of ecosystems—forests, freshwater systems, coastal/marine habitats, grasslands, and agricultural lands—are all showing significant signs of deterioration in many parts of the world. Many important ecological processes, such as the carbon cycle and water cycle, have been damaged by pollution. Linden concludes that humanity faces difficult choices in maintaining the planet's ability to support life.

As you read, consider the following questions:
1. How much of the world's wetlands and grasslands have been lost to human activity, according to Linden and PAGE?
2. What distinguishes the approach of the PAGE study, according to the author?
3. What important lesson can be learned from attempts to restore the Florida Everglades, according to Linden?

For more than 40 years, earth has been sending out distress signals. At first they were subtle, like the thin shells of bald-eagle eggs that cracked because they were laced with DDT. Then the signs were unmistakable, like the pall of smoke over the Amazon rain forest, where farmers and ranchers set fires to clear land. Finally, as the new millennium drew near, it was obvious that Earth's pain had become humanity's pain. The collapse of the North Atlantic cod fishery put 30,000 Canadians out of work and ruined the economies of 700 communities. Two years ago, deforestation worsened China's floods, which killed 3,600 people and left 14 million homeless. Population pressures and overcrowding raised the toll from last year's rains in Latin America, which killed more than 30,000 people and created armies of environmental refugees.

And how have we responded to four decades of ever louder distress signals? We've staged a procession of Earth Days, formed Green parties, passed environmental laws, forged a few international treaties and organized global gabfests and photo ops like the 1992 Earth Summit in Rio de Janeiro. All the while, the decline of Earth's ecosystems has continued unabated.

What will it take for us to get serious about saving our environment? When will environmentalism move from being a philosophy promoted by a passionate minority to a way of life that governs mainstream behavior and policy? How can we understand that Earth is one big natural system and that torching tropical rain forests and destroying coral reefs will eventually threaten the well-being of towns and cities everywhere?

One crucial step is a true accounting of the state of the planet, a thorough assessment of the health of all Earth's major ecosystems, from oceans to forests. Only a comprehensive global survey can show how damage to one system is affecting other systems and can determine whether Earth as a whole is losing its ability to nurture the full diversity of life and the economies of nations.

That was the thinking behind the launching of the most ambitious study of global ecosystems ever undertaken. In September, at a special millennial session of the U.N., four of its agencies and partners—the World Bank, the U.N. Development Program, the U.N. Environment Program and the World Resources Institute—will present the first results of this project, a Pilot Analysis of Global Ecosystems. The findings of the $4 million study, called PAGE for short, will be published in the 2000–01 edition of the *World Resources Report* titled *People and Ecosystems: The Fraying Web of Life*. . . . The goal is to answer the most important question of the century: What is happening to Earth's capacity to support nature and civilization?

Time was given an exclusive advance look at the U.N. report, which makes for sobering reading. Its conclusions are divided into assessments of five major types of ecosystems—forests, freshwater systems, coastal/marine habitats, grasslands and agricultural lands—and all five are showing signs of deterioration. The report's maps and charts capture the stunning scale and character of human impact on the planet. One set reveals the degree to which agricultural lands have been degraded around the world by the buildup of salts and the loss of nutrients; another locates oceanic dead zones caused by pollutants flowing to the sea from rivers; another shows the degree to which productive parts of the sea floor have been destroyed by trawling; another highlights how much humanity has altered coastlines. Many of the statistics are staggering: half the world's wetlands have been lost in the past century; 58% of coral reefs are imperiled by human activity; 80% of grasslands are suffering from soil degradation; 20% of drylands are in danger of becoming deserts; and groundwater is being depleted almost everywhere.

But as dramatic as these numbers are, will PAGE accomplish anything? The U.N. has a reputation for studying problems as a substitute for doing something about them. Its agencies churn out paper the way ragweed produces pollen, and most U.N. studies quickly disappear into file-cabinet oblivion in the offices of other paper shufflers. Moreover, after decades of conferences on environment and sustainable development, the natural response to such an assessment is, "Hasn't someone already done this?"

No, nothing this sweeping. PAGE brought together 175 scientists from many disciplines and nations. They drew upon, reanalyzed and integrated the data collected in roughly 100 prior assessments and studies of various ecosystems and regions. They also pored over new findings collected through satellite imaging and other forms of remote sensing. The purpose was to identify gaps in information, target critical areas deserving attention and pinpoint likely trouble spots in the future. . . .

PAGE is the first time a critical mass of scientists from different disciplines has rallied around the crisis in the planet's ecosystems. Notes Calestous Juma of Harvard's Kennedy School of Government: "If you look at issues like ozone depletion and climate change, there was progress because different scientists pulled together in assessments. That hasn't happened until now in biological systems."

Nature the Producer

What really distinguishes PAGE is its approach. It's significant that two of the sponsoring agencies—the U.N. Development Program and the World Bank—deal primarily with economic development. Their participation acknowledges an inescapable fact: economies cannot remain forever healthy in an unhealthy environment. PAGE looks at the natural world in a new way: not just as a beautiful place that should be preserved for aesthetic or moral reasons but also as an economic asset that delivers irreplaceable goods and services. Ecosystems temper climate, purify and store water, recycle wastes, produce food and support all the other things that make Earth a friendly oasis in a stark and lonely universe. Despite the universally acknowledged importance of these life-creating natural networks, until now no organization has undertaken a global assessment of Earth's capacity to continue delivering goods and services.

PAGE starkly concludes that our planet's capacity is beginning to diminish, threatening our economic well-being and ultimately our survival. It's not possible to go through the report's maps, charts, graphs and case studies without wondering, How did we let things get to this point?

The answer lies in a paradox. No one argues that life on Earth would be possible without ecosystems, but the entire march of human progress has occurred against a backdrop of landscapes transformed from their natural state to suit the needs of agriculture and industry. Various societies have degraded huge areas without suffering dire consequences. In the U.S., pioneers plowed up almost the entire prairie on the nation's way to becoming an agricultural and economic colossus, but America lost what may have been the greatest concentration of animal life on the planet. Britain, Japan, Korea and Thailand are among the societies that prospered even as they converted their original natural systems into farms and industrial parks, diverted and despoiled their rivers and re-engineered their coasts.

The world needs ecosystems, but apparently not every ecosystem, everywhere. The genius of the market economy is that it enables a nation to buy from other places or re-create through technology some of the benefits once derived from the local habitat. The genius of nature is that ecosystems can absorb shocks and sustain damage and still rebound.

Outstripping Capacity

One reason governments have been slow to respond to the environmental crisis is that Earth is still churning out plenty of goods—enough fiber, grain and fish to support 6 billion people. Many are malnourished, of course, but that's primarily a matter of bad distribution. A closer look at the trends, though, is disturbing. PAGE points out that there is a difference between current production and capacity, which is the amount of grain or fish the globe can produce indefinitely. Fishing fleets, the report says, are 40% larger than the ocean can sustain. At that rate, more fisheries are bound to collapse, as did the North Atlantic cod grounds. We're borrowing heavily from our children's future.

Consider the situation in Africa's Lake Victoria. A superficial look at production shows a rosy picture of a giant lake producing 300,000 metric tons of Nile perch and tilapia annually, yielding roughly $300 million in the export market. The two fish are not native, however, and introducing these species has jeopardized the dynamics of Africa's largest lake. The invaders have crowded out 350 species of native cichlid fish that used to support the local fishermen, most of whom cannot afford the equipment necessary to fish for perch. With the cichlid population reduced more than 80%, malnutrition is more evident in surrounding villages, even as the export market booms.

The perch-tilapia takeover has upset the system in other ways as well. Without the cichlids moving up and down the lake and mixing the waters, some layers of the lake are becoming stratified and depleted of oxygen. Algal blooms, fed by pollution and agricultural runoff, are increasing. All these changes have taken place in just 20 years. Now they are coming full circle; the lake's instability threatens the perch and tilapia fishery.

Can Earth Absorb More People?

Whether Earth has the ability to absorb more people and provide for their ever-growing needs is not a closed question. Some technocrats have argued that the Earth's greatest resource is the innate capacity of human beings to invent or engineer their way out of population and resource crises. If that is so, however, human ingenuity is not keeping pace with human consumption as measured in the degradation of virtually every natural system—from the chilly North Atlantic with its vital fisheries to the steamy rain forests of Amazonia with their incomparable array of plants and animals.

When all is said and done, human activities caused by population growth and consumption patterns are taking a heavy toll on our planet's life-support systems—and on Earth's other species, which are disappearing at record rates as human numbers rise.

Don Hinrichsen, *International Wildlife*, September/October 1999.

Every ecosystem suffers from the kind of unintended consequences that jeopardize Lake Victoria. Shrimp farmers cut mangroves in Thailand, Ecuador and on other tropical coastlines, unaware that their increased production comes at the expense of offshore fishermen who catch fish nurtured in mangroves. Since 1970, global food output has doubled and livestock production tripled, but the trade-offs have been depleted, polluted water supplies, exhausted soils and destroyed habitats. Since humans already use more than half the available freshwater on the planet, and two-thirds of all agricultural lands is damaged to some degree, we face an enormous challenge merely to feed the 1.5 billion to 2 billion people expected to join the global population within the next two decades.

With so much at stake, you would expect nations to make the monitoring of ecosystem capacity a priority. In fact, another disturbing PAGE finding is that in many cases, the gap between what scientists need to know and what is available is widening, not shrinking. Access to satellite data has improved mapping of broad areas, but the report asserts that on-the-ground reporting on issues like water quality has decreased in the past 20 years. Indeed, the biggest gaps in information concern freshwater and coastal/marine ecosystems, which are in the worst shape and arguably the most vital for human well-being.

It is difficult enough to assess an ecosystem, but policymakers also need to understand how various ecosystems interact. Deforestation in mountains can worsen floods in grasslands or agricultural lands below, as was the case in China and more recently in Madagascar. Humans have hurt coastal/marine ecosystems directly by draining wetlands, cutting mangroves, trawling oceans for fish and destroying reefs and lagoons. But we also damage these ecosystems indirectly as rivers transport to the coasts the effluents and by-products of agriculture, industry, urban areas, logging and dams. As if all that weren't enough, man-made climate change threatens all coastal areas, as melting glaciers send more water seaward and the warming and expanding of the oceans cause sea levels to rise. Coastal cities may someday be inundated, and entire islands could disappear beneath the waves.

Upsetting the System

Anyone who has taken a general-science course knows that Earth's most important elements move in cycles, circulating from sky to land and sea and back again. The human presence has become so dominant that we have disrupted even these most basic mechanisms of the planet. Most familiar, of course, is what we have done to the carbon cycle. Because we are pumping carbon dioxide into the atmosphere much faster than land and seas can reabsorb it, the accumulating gas is trapping heat and upsetting the climate. The result is not only rising seas and fiercer storms but also a possible repositioning of the world's ecosystems as the boundaries of forests or grasslands shift. Many animal and plant species may not be able to adjust to sudden changes in their habitats.

Less familiar is the havoc wreaked on the nitrogen cycle. Through the use of fertilizers, the burning of fossil fuels and land clearing, humanity has doubled the levels of nitrogen compounds that can be used by living things. But those levels are more than can be efficiently absorbed by plants and animals and recycled into the atmosphere. These excess nitrogen compounds wash into fresh- and saltwater systems, where they produce dead zones by stimulating suffocating growths of algae. Since the global food system is based on aggressive use of fertilizer, restoring the balance of the nitrogen cycle poses a daunting challenge.

Even more devastating is what we've done to the water cycle. So large is human demand for freshwater that many great rivers like the Yellow in China and even the Nile in Egypt sometimes dry up before getting to the sea. When diverted water is returned to waterways, it often comes back laden with noxious chemicals and sewage. Moreover, the building of 40,000 large dams and many more smaller obstructions has converted most of the world's rivers into a series of interconnected lakes. Such a water system, like nothing seen since the end of the last ice age, has dire consequences for thousands of species adapted to free-flowing water. Human alteration of the water cycle also extends underground as farms and cities overtax aquifers, sometimes irretrievably damaging these reservoirs of groundwater as the land subsides and salt water intrudes.

Where's the Breaking Point?

Ecosystems are naturally resilient, but human impact can reduce their ability to bounce back in many ways. Rain forests withstand some degree of cutting, for instance, but once forest fragments shrink beyond some unknown threshold, the entire system loses its ability to recover. PAGE refers to a recent study led by the University of Michigan's Lisa Curran, who contends that human activities such as logging may have doomed Indonesia's great dipterocarp trees, the anchor of its rain forests.

These trees reproduce by releasing huge masses of fruit in a synchronized fashion that is designed by nature to overwhelm the appetites of fruit and seedeaters and ensure that there are always some seeds left over to sprout. The strategy, called masting, worked for millions of years. Now, however, the forests in Borneo have been so reduced that humans and animals can consume all the dipterocarp fruit, with the result that no new dipterocarp trees are taking root in the areas studied by Curran and her colleagues. Since a host of creatures ranging from the orangutan to the boar are dependent on the dipterocarps, the trees' disappearance may ultimately doom Indonesia's rain-forest ecosystem. PAGE scientist Nigel Sizer of the World Resources Institute notes that similar problems associated with fragmentation loom over all but the largest remaining forests on Earth.

Halting the decline of the planet's life-support systems may be the most difficult challenge humanity has ever faced. The report specifies some common-sense steps in the right direction. For instance, governments can eliminate the estimated $700 billion in annual subsidies that spur the destruction of ecosystems. In Tunisia, water is priced at one-seventh of what it costs to pump, encouraging waste. In the mid-1980s, Indonesia spent $150 million annually to subsidize pesticide use. With access to cheap chemicals, Indonesian farmers poured pesticides onto their rice fields, killing pests, to be sure, but also causing human illness and wiping out birds and other creatures that ate the pests. When Indonesia ended the subsidies in 1986, pesticide use dropped dramatically with no ill effects on rice production.

Corruption offers another target. PAGE notes that illegal logging accounts for half the timber harvest in Indonesia. Government officials have long looked the other way because of close financial ties to companies cutting the timber.

Mission Improbable

An ecosystem's intricate, interdependent webs of life are hard to restore once they have become frayed. The U.S. is learning this lesson in its multibillion-dollar effort to halt the decline of the Everglades, the "river of grass" that once covered 4,500 sq. mi. (11,700 sq. km) in Florida. Having spent much of this century channeling, damming and diverting Everglades water for urban and agricultural use, state and federal politicians have watched with growing alarm as these alterations threw the ecosystem into a tailspin. Wading-bird populations have plummeted; sport and commercial fish catches have fallen; 68 of the Everglades' resident species, including the manatee and the panther, have become endangered; and the capacity of the system to store water has shrunk even as human demand for it grows.

With Florida's water supply and a $14 billion annual tourist business in jeopardy, the Army Corps of Engineers put forward a $7.8 billion plan in 1998 to undo many of its earlier projects and restore the slow-moving sheet of water that made the Everglades a natural wonderland. Billions more will be spent removing phosphorus from agricultural runoff, restoring habitats and modifying development plans to reduce stress on the system, but there is no guarantee that even these efforts will bring back the Everglades. The unsettling prospect that the planet's richest nation may not have the wherewithal to restore a vital ecosystem underscores a theme that runs through the U.N. report and should guide development decisions in the coming years: it is far less expensive to halt destructive practices before an ecosystem collapses than it is to try to put things back together later.

In their joint editorial announcing the findings of PAGE, the heads of the World Bank, the U.N. Development Program, the U.N. Environment Program and the World Resources Institute confirm their "commitment to making the viability of the world's ecosystems a critical development priority for the 21st century." These are sweeping words, but the jury on this commitment will be composed of the world's ecosystems. The planet itself will let us know, in the harshest possible manner, if our words are not being backed by action.

*"The planet's ecological future has never
looked so promising."*

The Global Environment Is Not Deteriorating

Ronald Bailey

Ronald Bailey is the science correspondent for *Reason*, a libertarian magazine, and editor of *Earth Report 2000: Revisiting the True State of the Planet*. In the following viewpoint he analyzes the state of the world's environment and assesses the predictions made by notable environmentalists on the occasion of the first Earth Day in 1970. Bailey argues that most of the grim forecasts concerning population, pollution, and resource scarcity made then have not come to pass. He argues that the world has shown significant environmental improvements in the years between 1970 and 2000, and that technological advances and economic growth will enable the world's rich and developing nations to continue to make progress in protecting the environment.

As you read, consider the following questions:
1. What lesson can be learned from revisiting the prophecies of the first Earth Day, according to Bailey?
2. Why has pollution declined, according to the author?
3. What argument does Bailey make about the I = PAT equation?

Excerpted from Ronald Bailey, "Earth Day, Then and Now," *Reason*, May 2000. Copyright © 2000 The Reason Foundation, 3415 S. Sepulveda Blvd., Suite 400, Los Angeles, CA 90034. www.reason.com. Reprinted with permission.

Thirty Years ago, 20 million Americans participated in the first Earth Day on April 22, 1970. Fifth Avenue in New York City was closed to automobiles as 100,000 people joined in concerts, lectures, and street theater. More than 2,000 colleges and universities across America paused their anti-war protests to rally instead against pollution and population growth. Even Congress recessed, acknowledging that the environment was now on a political par with motherhood. Since that first Earth Day, the celebrations have only gotten bigger, if somewhat less dramatic: The organizers of Earth Day 2000 . . . expect 500 million people around the globe to participate. . . .

Earth Day 1970 provoked a torrent of apocalyptic predictions. "We have about five more years at the outside to do something," ecologist Kenneth Watt declared to a Swarthmore College audience on April 19, 1970. Harvard biologist George Wald estimated that "civilization will end within 15 or 30 years unless immediate action is taken against problems facing mankind." "We are in an environmental crisis which threatens the survival of this nation, and of the world as a suitable place of human habitation," wrote Washington University biologist Barry Commoner in the Earth Day issue of the scholarly journal *Environment.* . . .

Three decades later, of course, the world hasn't come to an end; if anything, the planet's ecological future has never looked so promising. With half a billion people suiting up around the globe for Earth Day 2000, now is a good time to look back on the predictions made at the first Earth Day and see how they've held up and what we can learn from them. The short answer: The prophets of doom were not simply wrong, but *spectacularly* wrong.

More important, many contemporary environmental alarmists are similarly mistaken when they continue to insist that the Earth's future remains an eco-tragedy that has already entered its final act. Such doomsters not only fail to appreciate the huge environmental gains made over the past 30 years, they ignore the simple fact that increased wealth, population, and technological innovation don't degrade and destroy the environment. Rather, such developments preserve and enrich the environment. If it is impossible to predict fully the future, it is nonetheless possible to learn from the past. And the best lesson we can learn from revisiting the discourse surrounding the very first Earth Day is that passionate concern, however sincere, is no substitute for rational analysis.

Population Fears

Imminent global famine caused by the explosion of the "population bomb" was *the* big issue on Earth Day 1970. Then—and now—the most prominent prophet of population doom was Stanford University biologist Paul Ehrlich. Dubbed "ecology's angry lobbyist" by *Life* magazine, the gloomy Ehrlich was quoted everywhere. "Population will inevitably and completely outstrip whatever small increases in food supplies we make," he confidently declared in an interview with then-radical journalist Peter Collier in the April 1970 *Mademoiselle*. "The death rate will increase until at least 100–200 million people per year will be starving to death during the next ten years.". . .

Although Ehrlich was certainly the most strident doomster, he was far from alone in his famine forecasts. "It is already too late to avoid mass starvation," declared Denis Hayes, the chief organizer for Earth Day, in the Spring 1970 issue of *The Living Wilderness*. . . .

Time has not been gentle with these prophecies. It's absolutely true that far too many people remain poor and hungry in the world—800 million people are still malnourished and nearly 1.2 billion live on less than a dollar a day—but we have not seen mass starvation around the world in the past three decades. Where we have seen famines, such as in Somalia and Ethiopia, they are invariably the result of war and political instability. Indeed, far from turning brown, the Green Revolution has never been so verdant. Food production has handily outpaced population growth and food today is cheaper and more abundant than ever before. . . .

Polluted Thinking

Pollution was the other big issue on Earth Day 1970. Smog choked many American cities and sludge coated the banks of many rivers. People were also worried that we were poisoning the biosphere and ourselves with dangerous pesticides. DDT, which had been implicated in the decline of various bird species, including the bald eagle, the peregrine falcon, and the brown pelican, would soon be banned in the United States. Students wearing gas masks buried cars and internal combustion engines as symbols of our profligate and polluting consumer society. The Great Lakes were in bad shape and Lake Erie was officially "dead," its fish killed because oxygen supplies had been depleted by rotting algae blooms that had themselves been fed by organic pollutants from factories and municipal sewage. Pesticides draining from the land were projected to kill off the phytoplankton in the oceans, eventually stopping oxygen production.

In January 1970, *Life* reported, "Scientists have solid experimental and theoretical evidence to support . . . the following predictions: In a decade, urban dwellers will have to wear gas masks to survive air pollution . . . by 1985 air pollution will have reduced the amount of sunlight reaching earth by one half. . . ." Ecologist Kenneth Watt told *Time* that, "At the present rate of nitrogen buildup, it's only a matter of time before light will be filtered out of the atmosphere and none of our land will be usable." Barry Commoner cited a National Research Council report that had estimated "that by 1980 the oxygen demand due to municipal wastes will equal the oxygen content of the total flow of all the U.S. river systems in the summer months." Translation: Decaying organic pollutants would use up all of the oxygen in America's rivers, causing freshwater fish to suffocate.

Of course, the irrepressible Ehrlich chimed in, predicting in his *Mademoiselle* interview that "air pollution . . . is certainly going to take hundreds of thousands of lives in the next few years alone." In *Ramparts*, Ehrlich sketched a scenario in which 200,000 Americans would die in 1973 during "smog disasters" in New York and Los Angeles.

So has air pollution gotten worse? Quite the contrary. In the most recent National Air Quality Trends report, the U.S. Environmental Protection Agency—itself created three decades ago partly as a response to Earth Day celebrations—had this to say: "Since 1970, total U.S. population increased 29 percent, vehicle miles traveled increased 121 percent, and the gross domestic product (GDP) increased 104 percent. During that same period, notable reductions in air quality concentrations and emissions took place." Since 1970, ambient levels of sulfur dioxide and carbon monoxide have fallen by 75 percent, while total suspended particulates like smoke, soot, and dust have been cut by 50 percent since the 1950s.

Being Optimistic About the Environment

You can be in favour of the environment without being a pessimist. There ought to be room in the environmental movement for those who think that technology and economic freedom will make the world cleaner and will also take the pressure off endangered species. But at the moment such optimists are distinctly unwelcome among environmentalists.

Environmentalists are quick to accuse their opponents in business of having vested interests. But their own incomes, their advancement, their fame and their very existence can depend on supporting the most alarming versions of every environmental scare. "The whole aim of practical politics", said H.L. Mencken, "is to keep the populace alarmed—and hence clamorous to be led to safety—by menacing it with an endless series of hobgoblins, all of them imaginary." Mencken's forecast, at least, appears to have been correct.

The Economist, "Plenty of Gloom," December 20, 1997.

In 1988, the particulate standard was changed to account for smaller particles. Even under this tougher standard, particulates have declined an additional 15 percent. Ambient ozone and nitrogen dioxide, prime constituents of smog, are both down by 30 percent since the 1970s. According to the EPA, the total number of days with air pollution alerts dropped 56 percent in Southern California and 66 percent in the remaining major cities in the United States between 1988 and 1997. Since at least the early 1990s, residents of infamously smogged-in Los Angeles have been able to see that their city is surrounded by mountains.

Why has air quality improved so dramatically? Part of the answer lies in emissions targets set by federal, state, and local governments. But these need to be understood in the twin contexts of rising wealth and economic efficiency. As a

Department of Interior analyst concluded after surveying emissions in 1999, "Cleaner air is a direct consequence of better technologies and the enormous and sustained investments that only a rich nation could have sunk into developing, installing, and operating these technologies." Today, American businesses, consumers, and government agencies spend about $40 billion annually on air pollution controls.

It is now evident that countries undergo various environmental transitions as they become wealthier. *Fortune's* special "ecology" edition in February 1970 was far more prescient than the doomsters when it noted, "If pollution is the brother of affluence, concern about pollution is affluence's child." In 1992, a World Bank analysis found that concentrations of particulates and sulfur dioxide peak at per capita incomes of $3,280 and $3,670, respectively. Once these income thresholds are crossed, societies start to purchase increased environmental amenities such as clean air and water.

In the U.S., air quality has been improving rapidly since before the first Earth Day—and before the federal Clean Air Act of 1970. In fact, ambient levels of particulates and sulfur dioxide have been declining ever since accurate records have been kept. Between 1960 and 1970, for instance, particulates declined by 25 percent; sulfur dioxide decreased by 35 percent between 1962 and 1970. More concretely, it takes 20 new cars to produce the same emissions that one car produced in the 1960s.

Similar trends can be found when it comes to water pollution. . . . Lake Erie once again supports a $600 million fishing industry. . . . The EPA estimates that between 60 percent and 70 percent of lakes, rivers, and streams meet state quality goals. That's up from about 30 percent to 40 percent 30 years ago.

Since 1972, the United States has invested more than $540 billion in water pollution control efforts, according to the Pacific Research Center. In 1972, only 85 million Americans were served by sewage treatment plants. Since then, some 14,000 municipal waste treatment plants have been built and 173 million Americans are served by them. Similar air and water quality trends can be found in other developed countries as well. . . .

Biodiversity

Worries about declining biodiversity have become popular lately. On the first Earth Day, participants were concerned about saving a few particularly charismatic species such as the bald eagle and the peregrine falcon. But even then some foresaw a coming holocaust. As Sen. Gaylord Nelson wrote in *Look*, "Dr. S. Dillon Ripley, secretary of the Smithsonian Institute, believes that in 25 years, somewhere between 75 and 80 percent of all the species of living animals will be extinct." Writing just five years after the first Earth Day, Paul Ehrlich and his biologist wife, Anne Ehrlich, predicted that "since more than nine-tenths of the original tropical rainforests will be removed in most areas within the next 30 years or so, it is expected that half of the organisms in these areas will vanish with it."

There's only one problem: Most species that were alive in 1970 are still around today. "Documented animal extinctions peaked in the 1930s, and the number of extinctions has been declining since then," according to Stephen Edwards, an ecologist with the World Conservation Union, a leading international conservation organization whose members are non-governmental organizations, international agencies, and national conservation agencies. Edwards notes that a 1994 World Conservation Union report found known extinctions since 1600 encompassed 258 animal species, 368 insect species, and 384 vascular plants. Most of these species, he explains, were "island endemics" like the Dodo. As a result, they are particularly vulnerable to habitat disruption, hunting, and competition from invading species. Since 1973, only seven species have gone extinct in the United States.

What mostly accounts for relatively low rates of extinction? As with many other green indicators, wealth leads the way by both creating a market for environmental values and delivering resource-efficient technology. Consider, for example, that one of the main causes of extinction is deforestation and the ensuing loss of habitat. According to the Consultative Group on International Agricultural Research, what drives most tropical deforestation is not commercial logging, but "poor farmers who have no other option for feeding their families than slashing and burning a patch of forest." By contrast, countries that practice high yield, chemically assisted agriculture have expanding forests. In 1920, U.S. forests covered 732 million acres. Today they cover 737 million acres, even though the number of Americans grew from 106 million in 1920 to 272 million now. Forests in Europe expanded even more dramatically, from 361 million acres to 482 million acres between 1950 and 1990. Despite continuing deforestation in tropical countries, Roger Sedjo, a senior fellow at the think tank Resources for the Future, notes that "76 percent of the tropical rain forest zone is still covered with forest." Which is quite a far cry from being nine-tenths gone. More good news: In its *State of the World's Forests 1999*, the U.N.'s Food and Agriculture Organization documents that while forests in developing countries were reduced by 9.1 percent between 1980 and 1995, the global rate of deforestation is now slowing.

"The developed countries in the temperate regions appear to have largely completed forestland conversion to agriculture and have achieved relative land use stability. By contrast, the developing countries in the tropics are still in a land conversion mode. This suggests that land conversion stability correlates strongly with successful economic development," concludes Sedjo, in his chapter on forestry in *The True State of the Planet*, a collection of essays I edited. In other words, if you want to save forests and wildlife, you had better help poor people become wealthy. . . .

Why So Wrong?

How did the doomsters get so many predictions so wrong on the first Earth Day? Their mistake can be handily summed up in Paul Ehrlich and John Holdern's infamous **I = PAT** equation. **I**mpact (always negative) equals **P**opulation × **A**ffluence × **T**echnology, they declared. More people were *always* worse, by definition. Affluence meant that rich people were consuming more of the earth's resources, a concept that was regularly illustrated by claiming that the birth of each additional baby in America was worse for the environment than 25, 50, or even 60 babies born on the Indian subcontinent. And technology was bad because it meant that humans were pouring more poisons into the biosphere, drawing down more nonrenewable resources and destroying more of the remaining wilderness.

We now know that Ehrlich and his fellow travelers got it backwards. If population were necessarily bad, then Brazil, with less than three-quarters the population density of the U.S., should be the wealthier society. As far as affluence goes, it is clearly the case that the richer the country, the cleaner the water, the clearer the air, and the more protected the forests. Additionally, richer countries also boast less hunger, longer lifespans, lower fertility rates, and more land set aside for nature. Relatively poor people can't afford to care overmuch for the state of the natural world.

With regards to technology, Ehrlich and other activists often claim that economists simply don't understand the simple facts of ecology. But it's the doomsters who need to update their economics—things have changed since the appearance of Thomas Malthus' 200-year-old *An Essay on the Principle of Population*, the basic text that continues to underwrite much apocalyptic rhetoric. Malthus hypothesized that while population increases geometrically, food and other resources increased arithmetically, leading to a world in which food was always in short supply. Nowadays, we understand that wealth is not created simply by combining land and labor. Rather, technological innovations greatly raise positive outputs in all sorts of ways while minimizing pollution and other negative outputs.

Indeed, if Ehrlich wants to improve his sorry record of predictions and his understanding of how to protect the natural world, he should walk across campus to talk with his Stanford University colleague, economist Paul Romer. "New Growth Theory," devised by Romer and others, shows that wealth springs from new ideas and new recipes. Romer sums it up this way: "Every generation has perceived the limits to growth that finite resources and undesirable side effects would pose if no new recipes or ideas were discovered. And every generation has underestimated the potential for finding new recipes and ideas. We consistently fail to grasp how many ideas remain to be discovered. The difficulty is the same one we have with compounding. Possibilities do not add up. They multiply." In other words, new ideas and technological recipes grow exponentially at a rate much faster than population does. . . .

What will Earth look like when Earth Day 60 rolls around in 2030? Here are my predictions: As the International Food Policy Research Institute projects, we will be able to feed the world's additional numbers and to provide them with a better diet. Because they are ultimately political in nature, poverty and malnutrition will not be eliminated, but economic growth will make many people in the developing world much better off. Technological improvements in agriculture will mean less soil erosion, better management of freshwater supplies, and higher productivity crops. Life expectancy in the developing world will likely increase from 65 years to 73 years, and probably more; in the First World, it will rise to more than 80 years. Metals and mineral prices will be even lower than they are today. The rate of deforestation in the developing world will continue to slow down and forest growth in the developed economies will increase.

Meanwhile, as many developing countries become wealthier, they will start to pass through the environmental-transition thresholds for various pollutants, and their air and water quality will begin to improve. Certainly air and water quality in the United States, Europe, Japan, and other developed countries will be even better than it is today. Enormous progress will be made on the medical front, and diseases like AIDS and malaria may well be finally conquered. As for climate change, concern may be abating because the world's energy production mix is shifting toward natural gas and nuclear power. There is always the possibility that a technological breakthrough—say, cheap, efficient, non-polluting fuel cells—could radically reshape the energy sector. In any case a richer world will be much better able to cope with any environmental problems that might crop up.

One final prediction, of which I'm most absolutely certain: There will be a disproportionately influential group of doomsters predicting that the future—and the present—never looked so bleak.

*"The planet is heating at a faster rate than
at any time in the last 10,000 years."*

Global Warming Is a Serious Environmental Threat

Ross Gelbspan

Ross Gelbspan is a Pulitzer Prize–winning journalist and author of *The Heat Is On: The Climate Crisis, The Cover-up, the
Prescription*. In the following viewpoint, he argues that the
global climate is gradually warming. A cause of this heating,
he asserts, is the millions of tons of gases such as carbon
dioxide that humans pump into the atmosphere by burning
fossil fuels. These gases trap heat, raise the average global
temperature, and indirectly cause many negative effects, including floods, storms, and droughts. Gelbspan argues that
the corporations that produce fossil fuels are attempting to
convince the public that there is no climate crisis, but their
claims are not supported by the available evidence.

As you read, consider the following questions:

1. What are some of the small, medium, and large
   phenomena that Gelbspan attributes to global warming?
2. What responses does the author make to those who
   question the significance of global warming?
3. What solution to global warming does Gelbspan
   propose?

Excerpted from Ross Gelbspan, "The Global Warming Crisis," *Yes!*, Winter
1999/2000. Reprinted with permission from *Yes! A Journal of Positive Futures*,
PO Box 10818, Bainbridge Island, WA 98110. Subscriptions: 1-800-937-4451;
website: www.futurenet.org.

In 1997, hikers found hundreds of seal pups dying of starvation on the beaches of northern California. Investigators concluded the pups were starving because the fish on which they feed were driven to depths beyond the range of the young seals by warming surface waters. Last July's intense heat wave [of 1999] in the Northeastern United States accelerated demands for air conditioning, causing blackouts and brownouts around the country. In Oswego, New York, home of the Fitzpatrick nuclear power plant, electrical service was cut back—but for a different reason. Atmospheric heating had made the surface water of Lake Ontario so warm it was no longer able to provide the requisite cooling for the power plant.

In the spring of 1998, when the storks were returning to northern Europe after wintering in Africa, they encountered a bizarre weather pattern. Northern Germany and Poland were caught in the grip of an extended spell of drought and frost. Their migratory instincts confounded, the storks turned back and began flying in wide circles over Turkey and the Balkans—until hundreds dropped out of the sky, dead from exhaustion.

In June 1999, the small, uninhabited South Pacific islands of Tebua Tarawa and Abanuea disappeared under rising sea levels. Researchers at the South Pacific Regional Environment Program said they feared that the nearby inhabited islands of Kiribati and Tuvalu would disappear as well. Disaster planners began to relocate residents to other, less vulnerable islands in the region.

These are some of the little signs of climate change.

Other Signs of Change

There are medium-sized and large signs as well. They include last summer's [1999] drought in the mid-Atlantic and Northeastern US—one of the worst in history; last summer's heat wave that killed more than 270 people in the Northeast; and the fires last summer that consumed one million acres in Nevada. They also include the Texas-sized Hurricane Floyd, whose severity was fueled by unusually warm surface waters in the Atlantic. Given the fact that warming has increased atmospheric humidity by 10 percent over the last 20 years—

accelerating the evaporation of surface waters and expanding the air to hold more water—it is not surprising that the nearly $1 billion in damages came primarily from the relentless rains that Floyd dropped over North Carolina and New Jersey.

Then there are the large-sized changes.

The southeastern half of the Greenland ice sheet—an expanse of land-bound ice second in size only to Antarctica—is thinning at an unprecedented rate, up to three feet a year.

Ocean surface waters in the eastern Pacific warmed by 2–3°F since the early 1970s, triggering a 70 percent decline in the population of zooplankton which, in turn, is jeopardizing the survival of several species of fish and large numbers of seabirds.

In Monterey Bay, California, ocean warming caused a turnover in the population of marine life, driving cold-water fish northward as warm-water fish and sea animals moved in to populate the area. At the same time, atmospheric warming has propelled whole populations of butterflies from the mountains of Mexico to the hills of Vancouver, as they relocated north to escape the warming of their traditional habitats.

Warming has also been detected in the deep oceans. That is causing the break up of Antarctic ice shelves—another piece of the Larsen Ice Shelf the size of Connecticut broke off in March 1998. It appears that same ocean warming, together with rising air temperatures in Antarctica, will also double in the next century. (Our current level of 360 parts per million (ppm) of CO_2 is already higher than at any time during the past 400,000 years.) An intermediate concentration of 450 ppm, which most experts regard as inevitable within the next 70 years, correlates with an increase in the global temperature of 3° to 7°F. By contrast, the last Ice Age was only 5° to 9°F colder than our current climate. Each year, we are pumping nearly seven billion tons of heat-trapping carbon into our atmosphere whose outer extent is only about 12 miles overhead.

As a consequence, the 11 hottest years in recorded history have occurred since 1980. The period from 1991 to 1995 constitutes the hottest five-year period on record. 1998 just replaced 1997 as the hottest year in recorded history. The decade of the 1990s is the hottest in this millennium. The planet is heating at a faster rate than at any time in the last 10,000 years.

Extreme Weather

Even more evident than the increase in temperature is the increase in extreme weather events—and the growing destabilization of the global climate. To cite a few examples from the last few years:

In 1997, we saw:

- major damage from a succession of ice and rain storms in the Pacific Northwest in January;
- the heaviest rains in 30 years in Bolivia in February which destroyed half that country's crops;
- record flooding in March along the Ohio River;
- in Portugal, the worst winter drought in 150 years, which destroyed 70 percent of the country's winter cereal crops;
- epic April flooding of the Red River in North Dakota and Manitoba;
- a torrential rainfall in Manila in May that left 120,000 people homeless;
- the worst drought in 100 years in Chile, followed by torrential downpours which dumped six months' worth of rain in a week;
- the worst flooding in a century along the Oder River in Poland and the Czech Republic;
- 2,500 dead and missing in Southeast Asia as a result of Typhoon Linda in early November, a storm which Vietnamese officials called the "calamity of the century";
- 2,000 people killed and 200,000 made homeless in Somalia and Ethiopia by the worst flooding in memory in early December;
- Moscow's coldest December in 115 years which followed the warmest December in Moscow's history the previous year;
- my own Boston weather in which a 60-degree Easter Sunday was followed two days later by a 30-inch snowstorm—the third largest snowfall in Boston's history.

The next year, 1998, began with an extraordinary ice storm which immobilized parts of northern New England

and Quebec for a month. That year brought us the fires in Brazil and Mexico (in which, for the first time, rainforests caught fire) as well as Florida. It triggered killer heat waves in Texas, the Middle East, and India, where some 5,000 people died of heat effects. It produced Mexico's worst drought in 70 years; flooding in China that left 14 million people homeless; the worst flooding in the history of Bangladesh, which left some 30 million people homeless; and the 9,000 casualties in Central America from Hurricane Mitch, the strongest Atlantic tropical storm in 200 years.

While these examples are anecdotal, they are precisely the kinds of extreme weather events the current generation of computer models project as the early stages of global warming.

Financially, the consequences are visible in the rising disaster relief costs to government and escalating losses to the world's property insurers. During the 1980s, those insurance losses due to extreme weather events averaged $2 billion a year; in the 1990s they [averaged] $12 billion a year. In fact, the $89 billion in losses to extreme events in 1998 alone exceeds the total losses for the entire decade of the 1980s. In July 1999, the National Oceanic and Atmospheric Administration (NOAA) reported that in the last 20 years, the US alone has absorbed 42 extreme weather events that resulted in losses exceeding $1 billion each. As the insurance giant, Munich Re, recently reported: "The general trend towards ever-increasing numbers of catastrophes with ever-increasing costs is continuing." And the head of the Re-insurance Association of America has said that unless something is done to stabilize the climate, it could well bankrupt the industry.

Politically, there is a strong totalitarian threat to climate change. It is easiest to see in some of the world's poor countries whose ecosystems are as fragile as their traditions of democracy. It is not difficult to foresee governments resorting to permanent states of martial law in the face of food shortages, floods, droughts, incursions of environmental refugees and epidemics of infectious disease. . . .

The Skeptics

For many years, the public relations apparatus of big coal and big oil has argued that global warming was nonexistent.

Since 1991, the fossil fuel lobby has spent many millions of dollars to persuade the public, the media and policy makers that global warming is a non-issue. That propaganda campaign—especially as it was articulated by a tiny handful of scientists called "greenhouse skeptics" (many of whom received large amounts of undisclosed funding from fossil fuel interests)—centered on the claim that climate change was not scientifically proven. More recently, as the science has become too robust to deny, oil and coal interests have argued either that global warming is good for us, since it will enhance plant growth, or else that it is of no consequence because the anticipated temperature changes will be relatively slight.

Energy and the Climate

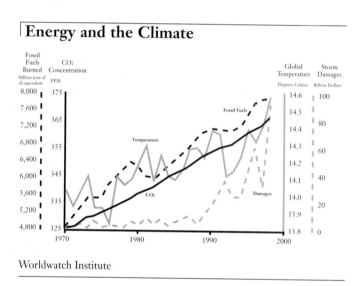

Worldwatch Institute

The arguments fly in the face of what we know about the planet.

The claim advanced by the carbon lobby that global warming will allow us to grow more food in the far north to feed an expanding population overlooks two elements. The first is the insects. Even a slight increase in warming will trigger an explosion of crop-destroying and disease-spreading insects. The second is that if the average global temperature increases by another half degree, it might promote some plant growth in the far north. But it would devastate crops in the tropical regions where most of the world's poor and hungry people live. It would cause large drop-offs in the rice yields of Southeast Asia, the wheat yields in India, and food crop growth in the tropics generally.

The second argument by the carbon lobby is more intriguing—that a small bit of global warming won't amount to any significant consequences. What is remarkable about that argument is that to date, we have seen only a small degree of warming—about 1°F over the last 70 years.

Yet even that small amount of warming is melting glaciers, heating the deep oceans, altering El Niño patterns, promoting the spread of disease, accelerating sea level rise, and triggering more extensive droughts, more intense floods, and more severe storms.

New Findings

New findings, moreover, indicate that the climate is changing much more quickly than scientists believed only a few years ago.

Tom Karl, chief scientist at the National Climatic Data Center, led a major research project which documented an increase in extreme weather events—including the fact that we are receiving substantially more of our rain and snow in intense, severe downpours than we did 20 years ago. When that study was published in 1995, Karl and his colleagues said they expected to see significant changes in extreme weather events in the next century. But they are seeing them now [1999]. The term "hundred-year storm" has no meaning any more, he said, noting that "we are now seeing hundred year storms every other year."

A study released in June 1999 by Dr. Tom M. L. Wigley for the Pew Center for Global Climate Change projected higher temperatures and faster rates of sea level rise than had previously been projected by the Intergovernmental Panel on Climate Change—a body of more than 2,000 scientists from 100 countries reporting to the United Nations. The study by Wigley, a pre-eminent climate modeler who is senior scientist at the National Center for Atmospheric Research, projected that by the end of the next century, the oceans will rise by 39 inches while Earth's temperature could

41

rise as much as 7°F. (Again, the last ice age was only 5 to 9°F colder than the current climate.)

The predictions for life on the planet a hundred years from now are extremely depressing.

Dutch researchers project that at current rates of warming, mosquito-borne diseases will double in the tropics—and increase a hundredfold in the temperate regions by late next century.

A team of Japanese researchers reported last year that at current rates of warming, 40 percent of the world's forests will have died by the same time. This would turn much of the globe's forested land from a sink (which absorbs carbon dioxide) to a source (which releases CO_2 into the atmosphere.)

Findings by researchers at NOAA predict megadroughts in the US near the end of the next century—while researchers at the US Geological Survey and the University of Toronto warn that such droughts could easily turn the wheat-growing areas of Kansas, Nebraska, and Oklahoma into deserts.

Scientists at Britain's Hadley Centre for Climate Change project that by late in the coming century, the number of people on the coast subject to flooding each year will rise from 5 million today to 100 million by 2050 and 200 million by 2080.

And a study by the Max Planck Institute in Germany projects that if nothing is done to slow the rate of warming, the world could easily enter a state of "permanent El Niño conditions" in another 50 years.

Ultimately, the most frightening scenario—and one that is the subject of increasing numbers of studies—involves what scientists call a "Rapid Climate Change Event."

Many prehistoric changes in the climate have happened as abrupt shifts rather than gradual transitions. The climate system is so delicately balanced that small changes have triggered very large outcomes. Many of those changes have come from what scientists call "feedback" effects—in which responses to events lead, themselves, to even more instability. For instance, higher temperatures promote drought and wildfires that, in turn, can burn vast areas of forest, releasing more CO_2, which would then accelerate the accumulation of greenhouse gases, leading, in turn, to more warming.

One of the most striking "feedbacks" took place about 10,000 years ago—and could, in the view of increasing numbers of researchers, repeat itself now—a "climate snap" that, paradoxically, plunged much of the world into a frozen, ice-covered state.

Near the end of the last Ice Age, there occurred a natural warming trend that increased the amount of snowmelt and precipitation in the far north. That infusion of fresh water diluted the saltiness of the North Atlantic. As a result of this dilution, the warming current (a.k.a the Gulf Stream)—which runs up the coast of North America, angles northeast across the Atlantic below Greenland and flows down the coast of Northern Europe—suddenly snapped and began to flow due east, as from New York to Spain.

With that change in the warming current, a deep freeze descended over Northern Europe. The climate of Britain became like the climate of Greenland. And what most astonished scientists is this: according to readings from ancient ice cores, that change occurred within less than a decade.

The Solution to Global Warming

The solution is as simple as it is overwhelming. To allow our inflamed climate to restabilize requires emissions reductions of 70 percent. And that implies a rapid global energy transition to high-efficiency and renewable energy sources. Those sources exist today, and they are capable of providing all the energy we use and more.

The good news is that a worldwide effort to rewire the planet with climate-friendly energy sources would result in an enormous economic boom. It would create millions of jobs all over the world. It would begin to reverse the widening gap between the North and South. It would substantially expand the amount of wealth, equity and stability in the global economy.

Alternatively, if we do not act quickly and comprehensively, the continuing succession of floods, droughts, storms, disease epidemics and insurance losses will tear holes in the global economic fabric.

And the planet may well lose its capacity to support the highly complex and organized form of life we call civilization.

"Any warming from the growth of greenhouse gases is likely to be minor."

Global Warming Is Not a Serious Environmental Threat

S. Fred Singer, interviewed by John F. McManus

The following viewpoint is an interview of atmospheric physicist S. Fred Singer conducted by John F. McManus. Singer disputes the contention that human activities are causing the global climate to warm significantly. Global temperatures fluctuate for many reasons, he argues, not all of them fully understood. Efforts to reduce greenhouse gases, as prescribed in an international treaty negotiated in Kyoto, Japan, in 1997, may harm the economies of industrialized nations but will probably have little effect on the world's climate. Singer heads the Science and Environmental Policy Project, a policy research group, and is a former director of the U.S. Weather Satellite Service. His books include *Hot Talk, Cold Science: Global Warming's Unfinished Debate*. McManus is publisher of *The New American* magazine.

As you read, consider the following questions:
1. What distinction does Singer make between the "greenhouse effect" and global warming?
2. What arguments does Singer make about the 1990 report produced by the United Nation's Intergovernmental Panel on Climate Change?
3. What are some of the possible benefits of a warmer climate, according to Singer?

Excerpted from John F. McManus's interview with S. Fred Singer, "Hot Topics, Cold Truth," *The New American*, January 31, 2000. Reprinted with permission from *The New American*.

J ohn F. McManus: *Do you have a position regarding global warming?*

S. Fred Singer: I certainly do. The climate warms and cools naturally all the time. It changes from day to day, month to month, season to season, year to year, and so on. At times, there is global warming; at other times there is global cooling. Some climate changes are predictable and some are not. We can predict that the winters are colder than the summers because we understand the mechanism. We cannot predict the climate from year to year, however, because we do not know why it fluctuates. When the climate warms, there could be a number of reasons for it doing so, including the sun. Another possibility is that human activities are adding greenhouse gases to the atmosphere, and this could produce some warming.

The important question then is: How important is the effect of human activities? And that we cannot tell. We know the theory, which says that human activity could be important, but the theory cannot be trusted until it has been verified. Until now, this theory, which is based largely on a mathematical model, has not been validated against observations. If the theory becomes validated against observations, then we can be more confident about using it to predict the future. But we're not there yet, and nobody should be basing conclusions and remedies on an unverified theory.

What do the scientific data really show about global warming?

Data from earth satellites in use since 1979 do not show any warming. But, eventually, they probably will because carbon dioxide and other greenhouse gases are increasing in the atmosphere. My personal guess, and I stress that this is only my guess, is that there is a greenhouse effect and that it is very small in comparison to natural fluctuations of the climate. We don't see this effect yet, but we may notice it in the next century. Even if we do notice it, it will be extremely small and actually inconsequential. It will be an interesting scientific curiosity but it won't be of any practical importance.

If we experience a couple of warmer years, is it possible that the next year will be cooler?

Of course. Climate fluctuates all the time, and we aren't always able to know why. During the period 1940 until 1975, the climate actually cooled. There was real fear that we were entering another ice age. But the climate suddenly warmed and these fears disappeared.

We repeatedly hear mention of the "greenhouse effect" in which heat is supposedly trapped in the atmosphere because of the presence of carbon dioxide and other gases. Is there such an effect?

Yes, there is a greenhouse effect. But the problem here is that high government officials have declared that climate science is "settled" and "compelling." The clear implication is that enough is known about it to act, and that any further research findings would be "policy-irrelevant" and not important to international deliberations that have led to a climate treaty. My published conclusions state otherwise, that any warming from the growth of greenhouse gases is likely to be minor, difficult to detect above the natural fluctuations of the climate, and therefore inconsequential. In addition, the impacts of warming and the higher carbon dioxide levels are likely to be beneficial for human activities, especially for agriculture that thrives on carbon dioxide.

But, again, the greenhouse effect is real. The emissions of carbon dioxide that we are putting into the atmosphere will make it more pronounced. But that doesn't mean that the climate is going to warm perceptibly. The atmosphere is very complicated, and there are negative feedbacks that cancel some of the warming. The easiest way to understand what I mean by "negative feedback" is to consider clouds. If you warm the ocean, you get more water vapor, more evaporation, and more clouds that will keep sunlight from entering the earth's surfaces. This results in a cooling effect—a negative feedback.

Reports about global warming repeatedly cite the 1990 report produced by the UN's [United Nations] Intergovernmental Panel on Climate Change (IPCC). Is this a reliable document?

The IPCC modified its own report after it had been approved, taking out key phrases to make it appear certain that human activities were affecting the climate. A few key individuals even removed much of the phraseology that discussed the uncertainties of such an opinion. Numerous scientists have pointed out that this document is unreliable.

Were the scientists who produced the initial IPCC report aware that changes had been made after they approved it?

No, the changes were done quietly by just a few individuals. Two thousand persons worked on this UN project and more than 1,000 of them were scientists. Approximately 80 saw and approved what they thought was the final report and then just a handful altered it. The newer version (in 1996) included a "Summary for Policymakers" containing a previously unmentioned factor involving human activity's effect on climate. This led to a conclusion that "the balance of evidence suggests there is a discernible human influence on global climate." Those who are skeptical about this IPCC conclusion have viewed the statement about "discernible human influence" as trivial and meaningless. But, on the other hand, the media and many policy experts have welcomed its convenient formula as scientific proof of a coming climate catastrophe.

Reprinted with permission from Chuck Asay and Creators Syndicate, Inc.

Did any of the scientists involved in this UN study balk at the alterations?

Yes, and perhaps the most noteworthy was the highly respected Dr. Frederick Seitz, the former president of the National Academy of Sciences whose objection was published in the *Wall Street Journal.* He became aware of what had been done and considered it a very grave breach of scientific protocol and ethics. He's been maligned ever since by individuals from the UN group and by others who decided to throw in their fortune with the UN. These people actually altered a graph and some of the text in the IPCC report.

There have been several articles about an increase in the number and size of icebergs that have broken off from Antarctica. Is the increase in icebergs due to global warming?

The climate did warm over the last 100 years and that's why icebergs are breaking off. There's no question about that. But the warming took place between 1880 and 1940 so that it is a bit warmer now than it was 100 years ago.

Does it take that long for an iceberg to break off?

Yes, it takes a long time for portions of the ice to break off. The melting has been going on for thousands of years and the West Antarctic ice sheet is still melting. The ice sheet may even disappear in 7,000 years. But the real point is that there's nothing we can do about it. The reason it's melting is because it's warmer now than when the ice formed a long time ago.

You mentioned the "climate treaty" and I assume you mean the 1997 Kyoto Protocol that called for industrial nations to cut emissions of "greenhouse gases" in order to deal with global warming. What is your response to this proposal?

The Kyoto proposal, even if fully implemented, won't accomplish anything as far as climate is concerned. It certainly won't stop the Antarctic ice sheet from melting. The only thing that will stop that is another ice age.

Won't it accomplish a great deal as far as industry is concerned?

Oh, yes. But the announced purpose of the proposal is to prevent global warming and stabilize the climate. It won't do anything of the sort. If you obey it punctiliously, and all the countries that are supposed to cut back their industrial activity do exactly as called for, even the UN group has calculated that it will reduce the temperature during the next century by 0.05 degrees. No one can even measure that! It is admittedly completely ineffective, so now they're saying that it's an important first step.

Do you see this as far more political than scientific?

Yes I do. Even a UN report says that we have to reduce emissions by between 60 and 80 percent worldwide. The

Kyoto Protocol, if implemented, reduces emissions by a mere five percent among industrialized nations only. But this would have a devastating effect on the economy of our nation. It's part of the anti-technology, anti-energy, anti-growth philosophy of the extreme "greens."

Have you seen or heard about the rash of television ads stressing the threat of global warming?

These campaigns are being underwritten by a few foundations. The National Environmental Trust has received $11 million to run ads. The government is doing its share by bleeding off money from research and putting it into town meetings and other gatherings to get people upset about this issue. Recently, there was a campaign in Minneapolis called "The Heat is On" to alert people in Minnesota to the *danger* of slightly warmer winters. That really takes the cake, doesn't it? I would think the people in Minnesota would be pleased if the climate warmed. The Canadian government has another program entitled "Environment Canada" to get the Canadian people to worry about slightly warmer winters.

Would it be harmful if the climate does become warmer?

If it does warm, there will be numerous benefits. Agriculture will be aided because crops will grow faster and sturdier. There will be slightly warmer winters with no effect on summers. Sea level will be hardly affected or perhaps it will rise slightly. This is because of the melting of the ice from the Ice Age and there's nothing we can do about it. Kyoto's proposals certainly won't help. . . .

Other than your own Science and Environmental Policy group, are you part of any scientific groups?

Yes, I signed the Oregon petition, which has been signed by 20,000 persons, 18,000 of whom have scientific degrees, many with advanced degrees. This project, begun in response to Kyoto, was launched by Dr. Arthur B. Robinson. He received important help from Dr. Fred Seitz, who sent a letter to scientists across the nation containing eight pages about global warming. In his letter, he stated that the Kyoto agreement was "based on flawed ideas" and that "data on climate change do not show that human use of hydrocarbons is harmful." And he urged recipients to sign the petition, which stated simply:

We urge the United States government to reject the global warming agreement that was written in Kyoto, Japan in December 1997, and any other similar proposals. The proposed limits on greenhouse gases would harm the environment, hinder the advance of science and technology, and damage the health and welfare of mankind.

There is no convincing scientific evidence that human release of carbon dioxide, methane, or other greenhouse gases is causing or will, in the foreseeable future, cause catastrophic heating of the Earth's atmosphere and disruption of the Earth's climate. Moreover, there is substantial scientific evidence that increases in atmospheric carbon dioxide produce many beneficial effects upon the natural plant and animal environments of the Earth.

The Oregon petition was never altered and has 20,000 signatories. The doctored IPCC statement has only 2,000 signatories. But the media seem to focus only on the IPPC statement.

What about the ozone layer and the claims that it is being depleted because of human activity?

The ozone layer depletion stopped about 1992. No more depletion has occurred. The total depletion that took place according to a thick United Nations report is about four percent. That's negligible. Ozone varies from day to day by about 100 percent, and from season to season—if you average it—by about 40–50 percent. The World Meteorological Organization and the United Nations Environment Program together produced figures stating that there has been no ozone depletion since 1992. . . .

Any final comments?

Ten to twenty years from now, younger people will look at their parents and grandparents in disbelief and ask, "Gosh, were you really worried about global warming and ozone depletion?"

> *"Just as cigarette companies long denied the link between cigarettes and cancer, so will the chemical industry deny that its poisons have a role in the cancer epidemic."*

Chemical Pollutants Are a Significant Cause of Cancer

Melanie Duchin

Since World War II, synthetic chemicals have played a growing role in industry and the manufacture of consumer goods. Some people have blamed ongoing exposure to these chemicals for the concurrent rise in cancer rates. In the following viewpoint, Melanie Duchin argues that the human body absorbs environmental chemicals, and that these substances are an important cause of cancer. She asserts that corporations have successfully influenced public discussion to focus attention on genetic and lifestyle causes of cancer rather than environmental factors. Duchin is an activist with Greenpeace, an environmentalist organization.

As you read, consider the following questions:
1. How have the odds of contracting breast cancer changed over the decades, according to Duchin?
2. Who does the author blame for not raising the issue of environmental carcinogens?
3. What criticism does Duchin make of government regulation of chemicals?

Reprinted from Melanie Duchin, "Ignoring the Roots of the Cancer Epidemic," *Greenpeace Magazine*, Fall 1997. Reprinted with permission from Greenpeace.

I have a personal interest in the latest news about the breast cancer epidemic. That's because, if I live a long life—which I fully intend to do—my chances of contracting breast cancer are one in eight. When I was born in 1961, my chances of contracting this dreaded disease were one in 20. That's a tremendous rise in just 35 years and odds that are not worth betting on.

What I hear in the media tells me that my risk of contracting this disease may be higher because I am an Ashkenazi Jew, I'm 35 and haven't had any children, I've never breastfed, and I started menstruating relatively early. On the other hand, I hear that my risk might be reduced because I exercise, eat a low-fat diet, and none of the women in my family have had breast cancer.

What I am confounded and angered by is the near total lack of coverage by the media and mainstream cancer organizations of the role carcinogens play in causing cancer. They tell me to practice breast self-exams, get a mammogram, eat low-fat foods, and stay fit. It's all excellent advice, but woefully inadequate. What I don't hear is the word "carcinogen," as in "reduce your exposure to carcinogens."

Because I work for Greenpeace, I have a professional interest in the breast cancer epidemic, and have files stuffed with information that make the link.

Unasked Questions

I know that my body has been subjected to an onslaught of carcinogens unlike anything my grandmother was exposed to when she was my age. As an average American, hundreds of chlorinated chemicals such as dioxins, PCBs and DDT have accumulated in my tissues. I grew up in an industrial section of New Jersey, yet when my doctor confirmed the presence of a lump I had found, she only asked me about my family history, whether I've had children and whether I've breastfed. She didn't ask if I grew up near a Superfund site, a PVC production factory, an incinerator, or any other source of carcinogens. She didn't ask if I played on a lawn that was sprayed judiciously with pesticides, or if I've been exposed to carcinogens where I work.

I don't fault my doctor for not asking these questions. I

blame the corporations that profit from the continued production of carcinogens, and who pay big bucks to public relations firms and lawyers to help shift the debate away from the role of carcinogens in causing cancer, and to protect their so-called "right" to continue producing these poisons. Just as cigarette companies long denied the link between cigarettes and cancer, so will the chemical industry deny that its poisons have a role in the cancer epidemic. It's in their best interest to ensure that the debate and research on breast cancer are focused on genetics, personal lifestyle choices and the search for a cure, while silencing or controlling any debate on preventing cancer through eliminating the production of carcinogens that cause the disease.

Thousands of Deaths

Suppose we assume for a moment that the most conservative estimate concerning the proportion of cancer deaths due to environmental causes is absolutely accurate. This estimate, put forth by those who dismiss environmental carcinogens as negligible, is two percent. Though others have placed this number far higher, let's assume for the sake of argument that this lowest value is absolutely correct. Two percent means that 10,940 people in the United States die each year from environmentally caused cancers. This is more than the number of women who die each year from hereditary breast cancer—an issue that has launched multi-million-dollar research initiatives. This is more than the number of children and teenagers killed each year by firearms—an issue that is considered a matter of national shame. It is more than three times the number of nonsmokers estimated to die each year of lung cancer caused by exposure to secondhand smoke—a problem so serious it warranted sweeping changes in laws governing air quality in public spaces. It is the annual equivalent of wiping out a small city. It is 30 funerals every day.

Sandra Steingraber, *Living Downstream*, 1997.

I also fault the government agencies which rely on a "one-by-one" approach to regulating chemicals. They effectively ignore the cumulative, combined and synergistic effects of exposure that many synthetic chemicals have. Cancer is just the tip of the iceberg in terms of human health effects from toxic exposures. Endometriosis, infertility, asthma and other illnesses are all on the rise, and all have roots in environmental contamination.

Protection Against Cancer

The American Cancer Society tells me that the best protection against breast cancer is to detect it at its earliest stage and to treat it promptly. I disagree. My best protection against breast cancer is to live in an environment that is free of chemicals that cause breast cancer. If the risk of contracting breast cancer can rise from one in 20 to one in eight in a mere 35 years, then it can drop as quickly, too. Those are the odds I'm betting on.

"There is no evidence that cancer in humans is linked to exposure to environmental chemicals."

Chemical Pollutants Are Not a Significant Cause of Cancer

Deanna L. Byck

Deanna L. Byck is the Director of Public Health Policy for the American Council on Science and Health, a private organization that provides information to the public on science and health issues. In the following viewpoint, she argues that environmentalist organizations have greatly exaggerated the role chemicals play in causing cancer. Little scientific evidence exists that establishes a link between trace levels of chemicals in humans and cancer, she asserts.

As you read, consider the following questions:
1. What reports and studies does Byck cite in her arguments?
2. What are the eight modifiable risk factors for human cancer, according to the author?
3. How do claims of chemical dangers harm public health, according to Byck?

Excerpted from Deanna L. Byck, "Health Views: Science Triumphs Over Toxic Terrorists," *Medical Tribune News Service*, September 11, 1998. This article is reprinted with permission of the American Council on Science and Health (ACSH), 1995 Broadway, 2nd Floor, New York, NY 10023-5800. Visit www.acsh.org to learn more about ACSH.

In September 1998, the *Journal of the National Cancer Institute (NCI)* confirmed that the apparent increase of brain tumors in children over the last 20 years is the direct result of our improved ability to detect them.

In actuality, there has been little change in the rates of brain tumors. With the help of technology, specifically high-tech screening devices, we're simply doing a better job of diagnosing them.

A Cancer Epidemic?

Yet the environmentalist community continues to warn us that the United States is experiencing a "cancer epidemic" and that chemicals are to blame.

The *NCI* report supports what many in the field of public health have long asserted: there is no evidence that cancer in humans is linked to exposure to environmental chemicals. In fact, it is the improvements in modern technology that enable us to detect and record cases of cancer more accurately than ever before.

The NCI researchers' findings illustrate why consumers should beware the frequent and unsubstantiated claims of the environmental doomsday crowd as it condemns products of modern technology, including agricultural chemicals, industrial products, pharmaceuticals and more.

A similar contradiction to the alarmists' conventional wisdom was revealed in [the] *Journal of the American Medical Association*, which published a study debunking the concept that mercury was detrimental to children's brain development. Researchers examined Seychelles Island children, who are known to have higher levels of mercury than American children. They found that these children scored higher than the general population on cognitive tests, indicating that exposure to this environmental pollutant was not a risk factor for impaired neurological development.

Eight Risk Factors

Decades of scientific research have identified only eight modifiable risk factors for human cancer. They are:
- tobacco use, particularly cigarette smoking

Cancer and the Environment

Many of the environmental concerns voiced by activists were, and continue to be, overstated. For example, while there is concern about the impact of industrial chemicals on human health, pollution appears to account for less than one percent of human cancer. A 1996 study by the National Academy of Sciences confirmed what many scientists have known for some time: synthetic chemicals, such as pesticides, in the human diet are not a significant source of cancer. People are at a greater risk for cancer as a result of unhealthy behavior, such as smoking or an unhealthy diet, than from industrial pollution.

Competitive Enterprise Institute, *Environmental Briefing Book*, 1999.

- alcohol consumption, especially in conjunction with to-bacco use
- overexposure to ultraviolet rays (sunlight)
- overexposure to radiation
- certain occupational hazards, such as long-term exposure to substances such as asbestos
- certain medicines, for example DES, which when taken by pregnant women increased the risk of a rare cancer in some of their daughters
- specific sexual and reproductive practices (having multiple sexual partners increases a woman's risk of cervical cancer; not having children or having a first child at a later age carries an increased risk of breast cancer)
- insufficient fruit, vegetables and grains in the diet

Leaders at the *NCI*, epidemiologists, and other scientists do not put exposure to trace levels of chemicals anywhere on this list of risk factors.

Public health professionals must respond to environmental groups that exaggerate chemical dangers and make unsubstantiated claims about increased cancer risks in order to prevent our scarce health-care resources from being diverted from real threats to pseudo-threats.

The best advice—beware of "toxic terrorists."

Periodical Bibliography

The following articles have been selected to supplement the diverse views presented in this chapter. Addresses are provided for periodicals not indexed in the *Readers' Guide to Periodical Literature*, the *Alternative Press Index*, the *Social Sciences Index*, or the *Index to Legal Periodicals and Books*.

Pratap Chatterjee	"Who Is Stealing Our Future," *Covert Action Quarterly*, Fall 1996.
Robert Costanza et al.	"The Value of the World's Ecosystem Services and Natural Capital," *Nature*, May 15, 1997.
Gregg Easterbrook	"Science Fiction," *New Republic*, August 30, 1999.
Economist	"Plenty of Gloom," December 20, 1997.
Paul R. Ehrlich and Anne H. Ehrlich	"Ehrlich's Fables," *Technology Review*, January 1997.
Environmental Health Perspectives	"The Environment and Cancer," July 1998.
Michael Fumento	"Good News, Bad News," *Reason*, June 2000.
Tina Hesman	"Greenhouse Gassed," *Science News*, March 25, 2000.
Llewellyn D. Howell	"Global Warming, Global Warning," *USA Today*, March 2000.
Thomas R. Karl and Kevin E. Trenberth	"The Human Impact on Climate," *Scientific American*, December 1999.
Bill McKibben	"Climate Change and the Unraveling of Creation," *Christian Century*, December 8, 1999.
Jim Motavalli	"Planet Earth at the Crossroads," *E Magazine* January/February 1999.
Kieran Mulvaney	"The Invisible Poison," *Greenpeace*, Summer 1998.
Arthur B. Robinson and Noah Robinson	"Some Like It Hot," *American Spectator*, April 2000.
Colin Tudge	"Planet," *Index on Censorship*, November/December 1999.
David T. Suzuki	"Saving the Earth," *Macleans*, June 14, 1999.

CHAPTER 2

How Can Pollution Best Be Prevented?

Chapter Preface

In an ecological context, "pollution" means the contamination of the natural environment by human activities. The term commonly refers to the fouling of air, water, and land by wastes such as motor vehicle exhaust, factory discharges into rivers, and roadside litter, but can mean any artificial contamination of an ecosystem. Humans have always created wastes that impacted their environment, but industrialization in the nineteenth and twentieth centuries created new sources and new types of pollution, including artificial chemicals and substances that had potentially severe environmental effects. In the early 1970s, amid mounting public concern over the environment, the U.S. government passed several laws that created the Environmental Protection Agency (EPA), which was empowered to set pollution standards and enforce federal pollution regulations.

Beginning in the late 1980s, writes Environmental Protection Agency official Odelia Funke, the concept of pollution *prevention* became increasingly important in environmental policy. Environmental officials realized that preventing pollution from occurring—as opposed to remedying or cleaning up pollution after the fact—can be a far more efficient and reliable way to minimize environmental damage from pollution. It is cheaper in the long run for companies to reformulate manufacturing processes so as to reduce the production of hazardous waste, for example, than to spend millions of dollars cleaning up contaminated sites later on. In keeping with this new approach, the 1990 Pollution Prevention Act established pollution prevention as a national environmental policy. Yet despite much agreement that pollution prevention is a worthy goal, disputes remain as to the best means to this end, especially on whether government mandates or private initiatives are superior. The viewpoints in this chapter examine some of these debates.

"Air pollution is just the kind of broad, all-pervasive problem for which federal regulations were designed."

Stricter Federal Regulations Are Necessary to Prevent Air Pollution

April Reese

The Environmental Protection Agency (EPA), an arm of the federal government, regulates air pollution under the Clean Air Act. In the following viewpoint, April Reese argues that although air quality has improved somewhat in recent decades as a result of government controls, pollution remains a serious problem that requires stricter regulation by the EPA. Air pollution endangers human health, reduces visibility, harms soil, and damages both wild habitat and city environments. The American public, she asserts, supports stricter air quality standards. Reese, a graduate student at the Yale School of Forestry and Environmental Studies, writes for *E Magazine*, an environmentalist publication.

As you read, consider the following questions:
1. What six pollutants were targeted for reduction by the EPA?
2. How does Reese respond to the argument that environmental regulations are too costly?
3. What actions should individuals take to combat air pollution, according to Reese?

Excerpted from April Reese, "Bad Air Days," *E: The Environmental Magazine*, November/December 1999. Reprinted with permission from *E: The Environmental Magazine*. Subscription Department: PO Box 2047, Marion, OH 43306; telephone: (815) 734-1242. Subscriptions are $20 per year.

On October 26, 1948, residents of the small town of Donora, Pennsylvania woke up to find themselves enshrouded in a stagnant cloud of pollution. Four days later, when the blanket of warm air that trapped the pollutants finally lifted, 20 people were dead and over half of the population—7,000 people—had become ill. Sulfur dioxide, nitrogen oxides and metal dust spewed forth from the four-mile-long local steel plant were the culprits.

Air pollution is one of the world's oldest environmental problems. By 1306, soot was so pervasive in London that the burning of coal was temporarily outlawed. Five hundred years later, in 1854's *Hard Times*, Charles Dickens described an all-too-typical cityscape of 19th-century America: "It was a town of machines and tall chimneys, out of which interminable serpents of smoke trailed themselves for ever and ever and never got uncoiled." In parts of the Midwest, the smoke and soot were so dense that the cities of Chicago and Cincinnati passed ordinances to control emissions from furnaces and locomotives, the nation's first air pollution statutes. In 1909, during Great Britain's industrial revolution, over 1,000 people died in Glasgow, Scotland because of smog. It was still a major problem 50 years later when, in 1952, 4,000 were killed by a week of London's "killer fog."

Now, on the cusp of the 21st century, we still can't breathe easily. Although air quality has improved over the past few decades, the Environmental Protection Agency (EPA) estimates that over 125 million Americans breathe unhealthy air—almost half of the U.S. population. Heart and lung disease aggravated by air pollutants result in as many as 64,000 premature deaths a year. Bad air causes more annual fatalities than car accidents. Every day, 14 people in the United States die from asthma. (Many are African-Americans, who die from the condition at a rate six times that of Caucasians.) Worldwide, air pollution harms the health of four to five billion people a year, according to a study conducted by Cornell University. That's more than two-thirds of the global population.

Children, who breathe in twice as much air as adults, are the most vulnerable of all. Dr. Philip Landrigan, director of the Center for Children's Health and the Environment in

New York, says that "Despite advances in therapy, asthma attack rates among American children have more than doubled in the past decade." Even worse, "Death rates are also rising," he says. Asthma is now the most common cause of hospitalization among American children, and the condition is becoming more prevalent among adults as well. As Ned Ford, energy chair of the Sierra Club's Ohio chapter, points out, "Even if you don't know someone with asthma, your insurance company does."

Something in the Air

We breathe once every four seconds, 16 times a minute, 960 times an hour, almost 8.5 million times a year. With each breath, we inhale hundreds of airborne substances, some naturally occurring, some the by-product of human activity. For those of us who live in cities—that is, most of us—many of those substances are pollutants that may increase our risk of respiratory problems and cancer. Smog, or ground-level ozone, aggravates asthma, and it can also reduce lung capacity and decrease the body's ability to fight off infection. Soot, or particulate matter, can cause bronchitis, chronic lung disease and irritation of the eyes and throat. Many hazardous air pollutants, such as vinyl chloride, arsenic and benzene, are carcinogens.

Even people who don't experience severe health problems from air pollution suffer in subtle yet significant ways. As Alfred Kneese wrote in the journal *Economics and the Environment*, the effects of airborne pollutants "range in severity from the lethal to the merely annoying." Not only can air pollution contribute to serious conditions like lung damage, bronchitis and asthma, it can cause nasal congestion, breathing difficulty, and can even prolong the common cold.

Air pollution is just the kind of broad, all-pervasive problem for which federal regulations were designed. Everyone breathes, so everyone needs to be protected from airborne pollutants. Congress finally recognized that need in 1970 and passed groundbreaking legislation to control emissions of air pollutants—with nary a dissenting vote. The Clean Air Act (the original version of which passed in 1963, but which didn't gain real muscle until a much stronger law was en-

acted in 1970, then reauthorized in 1977 and 1990) was en-
acted to protect human health with "an adequate margin of
safety"—a directive that EPA Administrator Carol Browner
calls "the most important provision of the Clean Air Act."

Air Quality Standards

The Act required EPA to establish National Ambient Air
Quality Standards (NAAQS) to reduce levels of the pollutants most harmful to human health. Six of the most prevalent and health-threatening air pollutants were targeted for
reduction: carbon monoxide, sulfur dioxide, nitrogen oxides,
lead, particulate matter and ozone. Standards were set for
each of these "criteria" pollutants based on the best science
available at the time.

In many ways, the new rules worked. Despite population
growth and a juggernaut economy, emissions of criteria air
pollutants fell 29 percent over the past three decades. Lead
levels, in particular, decreased considerably, thanks to federal
and state regulation. But concentrations of other regulated
pollutants (such as hard-to-control soot and smog) remained
high, knocking some areas of the country—like the east
coast, Midwest and southern California—into the "non-
attainment" dog house.

In 1997, recognizing that the standards it had set in the
1970s and 1980s were no longer sufficient to protect public
health, EPA drafted new NAAQS for two of the most harmful and persistent criteria pollutants: soot and smog. Soot
was originally limited to 10 microns, but the new rules
sought to control even finer particles, those at least 2.5 microns across. (These minuscule particles are dwarfed by even
the narrowest human hair, which is 40 microns wide. They
lodge deep in the lungs and stay there, causing long-term
damage.) Allowable levels of smog were reduced from 0.12
parts per million (ppm) to 0.08 ppm. (To get an idea of how
small this is, consider that one part per million is analogous
to one penny in $10,000.)

Most air quality experts agree that better standards for
ozone and particulates are needed. But are the 1997 standards good enough? "Yes, absolutely," says Frank O'Donnell
of the Washington, DC-based Clean Air Trust. "They were

an updating of the science and clearly would provide better health protection—and to more people." EPA says that incidences of respiratory problems in children alone would decrease by one million cases a year.

But sales of inhalers aren't likely to go down anytime soon. In May of 1999, in a case brought to court by a consortium of trucking, oil, and automobile companies and coal-dependent states, the U.S. Court of Appeals ruled that EPA shouldn't have been granted the authority to develop the new standards. Even though the Clean Air Act mandates that EPA protect human health with "an adequate margin of safety," the court said that tightening the standards to ensure that safety represented an "unconstitutional delegation of power." The decision flouted 64 years' worth of jurisprudence; the courts have consistently upheld EPA's authority in every similar case since 1935. Browner called the ruling "bizarre."

Jerry Taylor of the Cato Institute, a conservative think tank in Washington, DC, applauds the decision. "Congress has access to experts, just as EPA does," he says. "Congress should be responsible for making regulations." By shifting the burden of standard-setting back onto elected government officials, he says, the rules are more likely to represent the will of the people.

Yet the people seem content with EPA's role in the regulatory process. In a recent poll commissioned by the American Lung Association, 77 percent of respondents trust the EPA to set clean air standards. Only 51 percent trust Congress.

"That Congress chooses to delegate certain technical issues to an expert agency is a good, not a bad, thing," says Dan Esty, a professor at the Yale Law School and a former EPA assistant administrator. "We need our laws and regulations to be undergirded by more analytical sophistication, not less, as would be the case if Congress were called upon to set precise standards.". . .

Causes of Air Pollution

As the debate over EPA's new standards rages on, the question remains: Why are we still breathing bad air? The answer is a complex one, involving everything from regulatory shortcomings to industry subterfuge to consumer culture.

Without a doubt, industrial emissions are responsible for a large share of air pollution. In particular, coal-burning electric power plants are big polluters, accounting for 57 percent of the industrial pollution in the U.S. Unfortunately, they're now polluting even more. A study by the Environmental Working Group and the U.S. Public Interest Research Group found that coal use has gone up 13 percent.

Air Pollution Kills

Air pollution from the combustion of fossil fuels (oil, coal, and natural gas) in cars, trucks, and power plants, is killing roughly 60,000 Americans each year, according to researchers at Harvard University's School of Public Health. This represents about 3% of all U.S. deaths each year. Every combustion source is contributing to the death toll; none is benign, including incinerators; soil burners; flares and afterburners; industrial and residential heaters and boilers; cars; buses; trucks; and power plants. Diesel vehicles and oil- and coal-burning power plants seem to be the worst offenders.

The culprit in every case is the fine particles—invisible soot—created by combustion. Fine particles are not captured efficiently by modern pollution-control equipment. Furthermore, they are not visible except as a general haze. They are far too small to be seen. . . .

Why can't we act to prevent this important problem? Because U.S. regulatory agencies—and the courts—have lost their way, searching for the holy grail of scientific certainty. Regulators and judges now insist that science has to "prove harm" before regulatory control can begin. Philosophers of science know that science cannot "prove" anything. It often takes science decades—sometimes centuries—to reach a clear majority opinion and there will always be uncertainties, giving rise to nagging doubts, which can only be laid to rest by further study. In the meantime, . . . people are dying and children are getting sick because of fine particles.

Peter Montague, *Rachel's Environment and Health Weekly*, May 4, 1995.

When Congress deregulated the electric industry in 1992, old, "grandfathered" plants, which don't have to comply with the same standards as plants built more recently, gained an undeserved advantage in the new marketplace. "It's not fair for one plant to be subject to these rules and not another," says John Coequyt of the Environmental Working

Group. "It might have made sense at the time to grandfather some of these plants, but now, 30 years later, it's time for them to be cleaned up." That may finally happen, at least for some of the biggest polluters. In recent months, EPA has found that many of the oldest, dirtiest power plants, which have operated for decades within the haven of a Clean Air Act loophole, may have violated the law by expanding their power output without installing the necessary pollution control devices. The plants could be ordered to pay millions of dollars in fines and, finally, clean up their act.

Fossil fuel–dependent industries and states are sounding the now familiar alarm of financial ruin and mass unemployment as an inevitable consequence of tighter controls, warning that they "could deal a crushing blow to U.S. business." But history makes their claims dubious at best. The same "Chicken Little" argument is used every time new environmental regulations are passed or new standards are issued, but the cost of compliance rarely matches industry estimates. According to the Office of Technology Assessment, compliance expenditures for all environmental regulations combined amount to 1.5 percent of the U.S. gross national product.

Over the past 30 years, environmental rules have forced the development of new, cleaner technologies—often at lower costs than originally predicted. In 1994, four years after Congress passed the Clean Air Act amendments, [the oil corporation] Mobil admitted, "[We] opposed some of that legislation, because we thought it might be too costly for the consumer. In retrospect, we were wrong. Air quality is improving, at a cost acceptable to the motoring public." The estimated cost of implementing the new standards is about $86.5 billion a year. But the benefits amount to $120 billion, according to EPA. Esty points out that "Environmental protection investments always come at some cost. The question is whether the cost is worth paying." When it comes to the air they breathe, most Americans seem to think it is: According to the American Lung Association study, more than eight out of 10 voters want stricter air quality standards.

The Clean Air Act prevents EPA from considering cost when deciding on standards for air pollutants. Henry Waxman, a former Congressman from California and one of the authors of the 1990 version of the Act, is confident that the statute as written has succeeded. "In the Clean Air Act we've achieved what the public demands—economic growth and environmental progress," he wrote in a 1997 *Washington Post* editorial. . . .

Effects of Air Pollution

Human beings aren't the only ones who would benefit from stricter controls on air pollutants. In addition to threatening human health, ozone can stunt plants' ability to produce, grow leaves and store food, making them more susceptible to disease, insects and extreme weather. In high-ozone areas, yields of agricultural crops such as soybeans and wheat have been shown to be more susceptible to adverse conditions. According to EPA estimates, the new standards for ozone would reduce the yield loss of major agricultural crops and commercial forests by almost $500 million.

Air pollution can easily become water pollution. When sulfur dioxide (SO_2) and nitrogen oxides (NO_X) from burned fossil fuels mix with water and oxygen in the air, they form sulfuric and nitric acids. These acids fall to the ground in precipitation (not just rain), damaging mountain-top trees like spruce and acidifying lakes and streams. The most acidic rain on record fell on Wheeling, West Virginia in the 1980s. It had a pH of 1.4, making it almost as acidic as battery acid. Although things have improved somewhat since then, acid rain is still a problem. A National Surface Waters Survey found that hundreds of lakes in New York's Adirondack Mountains were too acidic to support a host of fish species. The survey also found that of the 1,000 lakes included in the study, 75 percent were affected by acid rain. Some lakes and their estuaries are completely barren of sensitive species like brook trout.

Polluted air can also wreak havoc on climate, impede visibility, contaminate soil, harm wildlife and damage buildings and monuments. In the 17 eastern states, annual air pollution damage to buildings and other structures—including the Statue of Liberty—so far has amounted to about $5 billion.

Grounded air pollutants can end up harming people, too. In fact, "a lot of air pollutants don't get into our bodies through breathing but through eating," says Sandra Steingraber, author of *Living Downstream*. "These contaminants fall onto the ground and land on plants directly from our garden or from the farmer's fields." She adds that we're also exposed to pollutants indirectly when we consume the meat of animals that were fed contaminated plants. "That's the lesson of ecology, that all aspects [of the environment] are interwoven," says Steingraber.

Electric utility plants powered by coal or oil (most often coal) account for about 70 percent of sulfur dioxide emissions and 30 percent of nitrogen oxide emissions in the United States each year. When car and truck exhaust is added in, over 20 million tons of SO_2 and NO_X are emitted into the atmosphere annually.

When fully implemented in 2010, the Acid Rain Program, passed as part of the 1990 Amendments to the Clean Air Act, will offer some relief. The 1990 Amendments require that the maximum release of SO_2 must be reduced to 10 million tons per year to decrease acid deposition. By lowering sulfate levels, the Acid Rain Program will reduce the frequency and severity of asthma, bronchitis and other respiratory conditions and will protect crops, wildlife, forests and buildings. The Program has aesthetic implications, too. Sulfate particles account for more than 50 percent of the visibility reduction in the eastern part of the United States, including national parks like the Shenandoah and the Great Smoky Mountains. The Acid Rain Program is expected to improve the visual depth in eastern states by as much as 30 percent. . . .

Getting to the source of a problem is always the best way to solve it. But past efforts to reduce air pollution have partly focused on measuring air quality in specific states and then requiring them to come up with a plan to improve it. Air pollution knows no boundaries, however, and states downwind from highly polluted areas were getting the short end of the smokestack. In the same way that rain from Ohio ends up drenching New Hampshire, "westerlies" push millions of tiny bits of airborne pollutants across hundreds or even thousands of miles. States downwind from heavily industrialized areas are saddled with the double whammy of their own pollution plus bad air blown in from afar. . . .

Ultimately, though, the quality of the air we breathe depends on us. By using our collective power as voters and consumers, we can reduce pollution, both directly and indirectly. We can choose alternative energy to power our homes, ensuring that deregulation of the utility industry improves the environment instead of degrading it further. We can buy cleaner cars, and let automobile manufacturers know that we care about what's coming out of the tailpipe. We can elect environmentally conscious government officials. Even simple, inexpensive actions can reap rich rewards: According to EPA, 175 pounds of carbon dioxide pollution a year can be saved just by replacing dirty air filters in air conditioners and furnaces. What to do with the old filter? Send it to your Representative as a reminder of how much farther we still have to go in cleaning up our air.

"*State and local governments may be better equipped than [the] EPA to address their own air pollution challenges.*"

Stricter Federal Regulations May Be Counterproductive in Preventing Air Pollution

Kenneth W. Chilton

In November 1996 the Environmental Protection Agency proposed new air quality standards governing ozone and fine particulate air pollution. The announcement stimulated much criticism of the EPA and debate over the efficacy of government regulations, and in May 1999 a federal appeals court ruled that the EPA had exceeded its authority in issuing the new rules. In the following viewpoint, Kenneth W. Chilton argues that the EPA's proposed regulations are expensive, and that the evidence that they would save lives by reducing air pollution is negligible. He argues that the EPA should take the costs of implementing regulations into consideration, and that state and local governments should have greater flexibility in determining air quality standards. Chilton is manager of environmental programs at the Center for the Study of American Business (CSAB) at Washington University in St. Louis.

As you read, consider the following questions:
1. What fundamental issues does Chilton say were raised by the EPA's proposed air quality standards?
2. What, according to Chilton, is the fundamental flaw of the Clean Air Act?

Excerpted from Kenneth W. Chilton, "Fundamental Issues Hidden in the Air Quality Dust Cloud," *Vital Speeches of the Day*, December 1, 1999. Reprinted with permission from the Center for the Study of American Business.

In July 1997, the Environmental Protection Agency (EPA) finalized air quality standards for ozone and fine particulate matter and hoped that it had closed the book on one of the most contentious chapters in its nearly three decades of rule-making. But the May 1999 remand of these standards by the U.S. Court of Appeals for the D.C. Circuit reveals that the issues involved are more fundamental than just a controversy over whether scientific evidence adequately justified new standards, and how costly the standards might be.

The most obvious issue raised by the appeals court decision involves how much authority Congress should delegate to federal regulatory agencies like the EPA. But another related question is whether economic costs as well as health benefits should be considered when setting air quality standards. A third issue, which may not be a part of this debate but should be, is whether the EPA should dictate air pollution remedies from afar or whether state and local officials should have more say. To better understand how these fundamental issues relate to the standard-setting process and to the appeals court decision, a brief review is called for. The EPA announced its plans to review the National Ambient Air Quality Standards (NAAQS) for ozone and particulates on June 12, 1996, and proposed new standards on November 27. By court order, the agency was required to complete its review of the particulate matter standard by July 19, 1997. Although the ozone standard was not on a similar schedule, EPA chose to review it simultaneously with the particulate standard.

At first, the debate was simple. Support for EPA's standards was led by "The Big E" environmentalists, the American Lung Association, and a handful of other interest groups. These organizations sought to portray any opposition to the high costs of tighter air quality standards as the usual blustering of big business. In fact, initial opposition did come primarily from the industries likely to bear the largest part of the burden of air pollution reductions, such as the petroleum, steel, automotive, and utility industries.

Soon governors, mayors, county officials, state legislators, and local air quality officers and commissioners also entered the fray. Some supported EPA, but many objected to the costs and disruption to current air quality planning and implementation processes likely to result from the proposals. Members of Congress from both sides of the aisle also took an interest in the issue.

After a significant number of Democratic representatives called for restraint, the White House began to take notice and requested that other executive agencies—National Economic Council, Office of Management and Budget, and the Council on Environmental Quality—participate in an internal review of the standards. On June 25, 1997, after much deliberation, President Bill Clinton announced his support for the standards. He did, however, modify the ozone and fine particle proposals to marginally reduce compliance costs and to allow more time before states would be required to submit fine particle implementation plans.

The Clean Air Act's Fundamental Flaw

Under the Clean Air Act, EPA must set air quality standards to protect public health "with an adequate margin of safety" against adverse effects. Taken literally, this means that air pollution must be reduced to a level where no one suffers any physical reaction. But because ozone causes some health effects in some individuals even at naturally-occurring levels, this goal is not possible to achieve. The Clean Air Scientific Advisory Committee, a group of scientists that advises EPA, tried to explain this to EPA Administrator Carol Browner in its closure letter on the ozone review: "Based on information now available, it appears that ozone may elicit a continuum of biological responses down to background concentrations. This means that the paradigm of selecting a standard at the lowest-observable-effects-level and then providing an 'adequate margin of safety' is no longer possible." The Clean Air Act also does not allow the EPA to consider economic costs when it sets standards for the six "criteria" pollutants—ozone, particulates, carbon monoxide, lead, sulfur dioxide, and nitrogen dioxide. Instead, the standards are to be strictly health based. Although this goal sounds laudable, it virtually ensures that for air pollutants like ozone that have no "threshold" level below which no physical responses can be detected, standards will be set too high, i.e., at a level where costs far exceed benefits.

Most economists would question the wisdom of ignoring the relationship between costs and benefits of public policy actions. Applying private and public sector resources to reducing air pollution when the added costs of doing so exceeds the additional benefits robs these funds from other potentially more valuable uses. "Compassionate" public policy calls for policymakers not to require expenditure of taxpayer or consumer dollars on problems whose benefits aren't commensurate with those expenditures.

Imagine buying a new car if your decision making were restricted similar to the bounds placed on setting standards under the Clean Air Act. You are to choose between a Chevrolet Corsica and a top-of-the-line Mercedes based on the single criterion of safety; you must not consider cost (after all, your children will ride in the car).

You would surely select the Mercedes. Only after your decision is made are you allowed to know the costs of the two cars. You might be able to find a low-interest loan or spread the payments over a longer period, but your safety-based decision would likely require deep cuts in other areas of your budget.

Given that you love your family members and care about their overall well-being, you may question the wisdom of basing your automobile purchase solely on safety concerns. Why not consider cost and safety at the same time? Indeed, why not consider other ways to provide better health for your loved ones than just automobile safety? If the Mercedes payments cause you to cut back on medical care or a healthful diet, your family's health has been harmed, not protected.

Costly Regulations

The costs of the proposed standards were hotly disputed, but all projections placed them in the range of billions of dollars. The EPA conservatively estimated yearly costs of between $600 million and $2.5 billion to partially attain the ozone standard and $6.5 billion to partially attain the particulate standard. These costs are in addition to costs to attain the existing standards.

Cost estimates for full compliance with the standards (which EPA did not provide) are much higher. The President's Council of Economic Advisers estimated that full attainment of the ozone standard would cost between $11.6 billion and $60 billion a year. Professor Thomas Hopkins, an adjunct fellow of the Center for the Study of American Business, estimated that the fine particulate proposal would cost about $55 billion a year to reach full attainment. . . .

The reason the costs are so high is that ozone and particulate levels in the United States are relatively low. From 1970 to 1997, emissions of volatile organic compounds (which contribute to ozone formation) declined 37 percent. Between 1978 and 1997, one-hour ozone concentrations fell 30 percent. Concentrations of particles with a diameter of 10 microns or less (PM10) decreased 26 percent between 1988 and 1997. As the air becomes cleaner, it becomes more difficult and costly to remove additional pollution. At some point, the cost of removing an additional unit of pollution becomes greater than the benefit derived from doing so.

Inconvenient and Ineffective Controls

The cost and inconvenience of the federal emission controls are increasingly being shouldered by consumers. Higher car prices, costlier maintenance, mandatory inspections and higher gas prices directly affect all drivers. The Clean Air Act also inflates the cost of many everyday goods and services and makes it difficult for corporations to expand and create more jobs in depressed urban areas. While federal emission controls are costly, they produce ever fewer environmental benefits and often come at the expense of more efficient and equitable approaches to air pollution.

Competitive Enterprise Institute, "Clean Air Act," *Environmental Briefing Book*, March 1, 1999.

The higher standards could represent a wise use of resources, depending on the size of the public health improvements that result. The EPA projects that a number of health benefits will result from lower ozone and particulate concentrations. These include fewer hospital admissions for respiratory ailments, and fewer cases of aggravated asthma, decreased lung function, respiratory symptoms such as cough and chest pain and lung inflammation.

The agency also estimates that the fine particulate standard would prevent 15,000 "premature" deaths each year. However, the health benefits are questionable. In an April

10, 1997 joint subcommittee hearing of the House Commerce Committee, Dr. Joe Mauderly, chairman of the Clean Air Scientific Advisory Committee, testified: "I do not believe, however, that our present understanding of the relationship between PM and health provides a confident basis for implementing a standard that necessitates crippling expenditures or extreme changes in lifestyle or technology. . . . We do not yet have a very good understanding of the biological plausibility of mortality from PM at the concentrations to which decedents were likely exposed. Our information from laboratory studies and our knowledge of the consequences of occupational exposures to particles do not suggest that people should die when exposed to PM at the levels indicated by epidemiology."

Assuming EPA's mortality benefits materialize, however, the lives saved would be mostly among elderly individuals with preexisting chronic conditions. The American Lung Association estimates that, on average, particulate air pollution reduces life expectancy by two years. At a cost of $55 billion to extend 15,000 lives, this represents a cost of $3.7 million for each premature death avoided, or $1.8 million per life-year saved. (Of course, the $55 billion also would provide additional health benefits such as fewer hospitalizations and incidences of cough and other respiratory symptoms.)

Without addressing the question of whether it is appropriate to prolong lives at a cost of $1.8 million per life-year saved, we can ask whether other public policy options could achieve the same health benefit at equal or lower cost. Research at the Harvard School of Public Health's Center for Risk Analysis found that 185 lifesaving interventions (regulations or expenditures) in the United States consume $21.4 billion in resources annually. These interventions prevent 56,700 premature deaths each year, saving 592,000 life-years at a cost of $36,000 per life-year saved—just 1/50 of the cost per life-year saved from EPA's proposed fine-particle standard.

The point of this comparison is that even if the optimistic health claims of proponents of the fine particulate standard are accepted at face value, the cost per year of extended life is far higher than other health-related government interventions. The opportunities for improving public health through the economy, rather than government action, likely are even more cost effective.

The White House Office of Information and Regulatory Affairs (OIRA) offers one estimate of the adverse health effects of well-meaning government intervention. OIRA estimates that each additional $7.5 million increase in regulatory costs results in one premature death. When individual incomes are lowered because of misplaced allocation of economic resources, the result is often lower living standards (i.e. nutrition, consumption of health care, and so forth) and, thus, lower life expectancies.

Current compliance with the Clean Air Act's mandate for setting health standards without regard to economic considerations is a "polite fiction." Standards are being set by the EPA administrator based on her implicit "feel"—judgment call—for "how clean is clean enough?" This is the act's fundamental flaw. And, in essence, it is this subjective carrying out of the Act's "mission impossible" that has run afoul of the nondelegation doctrine.

Federal vs. State and Local Authority

The process of setting new national ambient air quality standards for ozone and particulates also raised the issue of federal versus state and local authority. Not all areas of the country face the same type of air pollution chemistry or meteorology, so uniform national solutions are not likely to be the best way to deal with these problems.

As a result, state and local governments may be better-equipped than EPA to address their own air pollution challenges. It is a basic tenet of federalism that most problems are best solved by the people nearest to them, because they have direct knowledge of the circumstances. Even if air pollution standards continue to be set at the national level, state and local governments could be given a greater role in helping the EPA arrive at its decisions. The Clean Air Act leaves the development of implementation plans up to the states after the EPA sets national standards. Because it is their economies that will bear the burden, and their citizens who will enjoy the benefits, shouldn't states and localities have a greater voice in determining the level of the standards?

If states were given greater participation in the process, it is very possible that they would opt for standards less stringent than EPA's or for no change at all. Governors from 27 states and more than 1,000 mayors, state, county, and local officials expressed concern about the NAAQS proposals in letters to the EPA or to President Clinton. On June 24, 1997 at the U.S. Conference of Mayors meeting in San Francisco, nearly 300 mayors approved a resolution opposing the new standards. There was only one dissenting vote.

Clearly, state and local governments are interested in participating in the air quality standard-setting process. Placing all authority for setting standards with the EPA creates tension among the various levels of government. . . .

Zero Risk?

On the surface, Americans appear to expect that air quality standards will be set so that there is zero risk from air pollution. That is not surprising in view of the fact that we are repeatedly told by the EPA, environmentalists, the American Lung Association, and other public interest groups that this is our fundamental right.

But zero risk is neither a sensible nor a feasible goal. When air quality standards are set without regard to costs, the resulting policy does not serve the best interests of Americans.

What should we expect in the way of protection from air pollution? Rather than protection from any adverse health effect with an adequate margin of safety, the Clean Air Act should set standards "to protect the public against unreasonable risk of important adverse health effects." Furthermore, as a matter of good public policy, the Act should require, rather than proscribe, consideration of the tradeoffs associated with pursuing more restrictive ozone and particulate standards. Risk-risk comparisons and cost-benefit analysis are useful tools for this purpose. A virtual "zero-risk" approach allocates too many resources to small risks to the detriment of other, more pressing, needs.

In addition, a centralized decision-making structure allows for too little consideration of local or regional differences in air pollution problems. It also provides little or no voice for elected officials closest to the problems. These "in-the-trenches" representatives better understand the need to protect the environment using the most cost-efficient means.

Lastly, too much delegation of authority to a federal agency like the EPA further isolates decisions on environmental problems from economic and other important considerations. A delicate balance must be struck between delegated powers and retained authority. Too much congressional micromanagement of EPA can place the agency in "legislative handcuffs," denying the very flexibility needed to arrive at cost-effective solutions to these problems. Too much delegation can subject the nation to abuses of zealots who have little faith in private enterprise and too much faith in government decision making.

The most fundamental issue hidden in the air quality dust cloud is how to formulate public policy that is truly "compassionate." Because we care about promoting public health, we need environmental policies that do not consider risks from environmental contaminants in isolation. Rather than sitting on the sidelines watching the appeals process play out, Congress should amend the Clean Air Act to truly benefit all Americans.

"The environment would certainly benefit if many of the products now made from virgin resources were manufactured from recycled resources instead."

Recycling Is an Effective Means of Preventing Solid Waste Pollution

Allen Hershkowitz

Recycling involves using selected materials from garbage in the manufacture of new products, rather than burying the garbage in a landfill or burning it in an incinerator. In the following viewpoint, Allen Hershkowitz argues that recycling is a highly effective means of reducing pollution and conserving natural resources, and should be further encouraged. Recycling prevents garbage from being placed in landfills that may cause land and water pollution, he asserts. Hershkowitz is a senior scientist with the National Resources Defense Council, an environmentalist organization.

As you read, consider the following questions:
1. What in Hershkowitz's view are some of the environmental problems associated with landfills?
2. How have recycling programs affected landfill capacity, according to the author?
3. How do the expenses of curbside recycling programs compare with those of trash disposal programs, according to Hershkowitz?

Reprinted from Allen Hershkowitz, "Critics Willing to Throw Away Proven Success," *San Diego Union-Tribune*, September 21, 1997. Reprinted with permission from the author.

A small but vocal chorus of anti-environmental interests has tried to cast doubt on the value of recycling, perhaps the most widely practiced and most basic of all environmental policies. . . .

[A] prominent attack on the nation's growing commitment to recycling was a lengthy cover story, "Recycling Is Garbage," published in the *New York Times Magazine* on June 30, 1996. In it, John Tierney, a staff writer for the magazine, argued that most recycling efforts are economically unsound and of questionable environmental value. Tierney described recycling as perhaps "the most wasteful activity in modern America."

The article was a challenge to all Americans committed to environmental protection. Obviously, not all the materials found in the municipal waste stream can be recycled, nor can all consumer products be made from recycled materials. But the United States is far from those practical limits. A much higher percentage of materials now discarded in the U.S. waste stream can he recycled, and the environment would certainly benefit if many of the products now made from virgin resources were manufactured from recycled resources instead.

Virtually every issue put forth by those who take the anti-recycling position has been subject to thorough review and debate, producing volumes of research. Rarely do the facts support the anti-recycling stance.

Less Garbage

The most obvious and well-known advantage of recycling is that it leads to less garbage being buried in landfills, and environmental problems are the major reason more than 10,000 landfills have closed in the United States in the past 15 years [prior to 1997].

Landfills are neither simple, cheap, nor environmentally safe. Landfills generate hazardous and uncontrolled air emissions and also threaten surface and ground-water supplies. Landfills have contaminated aquifer drinking water supplies, wetlands, and streams throughout the United States—indeed, throughout the world—and many continue to do so. The list of toxic and hazardous chemicals emitted as gas or leaching as liquid from literally thousands of landfills defines a waste management option with wide-ranging pollution impacts.

More significant, and again contrary to the impression one gets from reading anti-recycling reports, even those landfills that use liners to protect against subsurface water pollution report troubling problems. A summary of industry experience with landfill liner technology drew the following conclusions: "Early experience in the use of geomembrane-lined sites showed that many, many leaked. More recent experience indicates that even with strict construction quality assurance supervision, many still leaked."

In addition to mistakenly claiming that landfills are environmentally safe, those who argue against recycling contend that landfill space is widely available and cheap. According to the Reason Foundation, "The landfill crisis is a political crisis, not an environmental one."

Landfill Capacity

The three most substantial reasons accounting for the increase in landfill availability are:

• Recycling has grown and now diverts almost 24 percent of the nation's municipal waste stream to other, economically productive uses.

• Developers invested in new landfill capacity, anticipating very high financial returns as thousands of facilities closed due to environmental problems.

• Recycling of yard waste has grown from virtually zero to 20 percent between 1985 and 1993. Recycling thus accounts for two of the three most important causes that have produced new landfill capacity.

The number of states with landfill capacity extending beyond the next five years rose slightly, from 42 in 1986 to 48 in 1995. Viewed from this national perspective, existing landfill capacity in the United States today is not all that different from that in 1986.

What has changed since 1986 is that thousands of environmentally dangerous landfills have closed, so the proximity of landfills to waste generators has been reduced. This results in more vehicle miles traveled to dump garbage, more costly time on the road for haulers, increased wear and tear on trucks, etc. According to the National Solid Waste Management Association, from 1988 to 1991 the number of landfills in the United States declined by 4,682 or 62 percent.

Even if landfill capacity were as cheap and available as some insist it is, it would be unwise to bury valuable, already refined materials that took energy, resources, and money to produce when instead they can be productively recycled.

Compared with traditional garbage collection, expenditures on recycling efforts are invariably smaller and offer the potential to generate their own revenue stream, even if they do not always break even. As Michael Shapiro, the EPA's director of the Office of Solid Waste, observed:

The Case for Recycling

The case for recycling is strong. The bottom line is clear. Recycling requires a trivial amount of our time. Recycling saves money and reduces pollution. Recycling creates more jobs than landfilling or incineration. And a largely ignored but very important consideration, recycling reduces our need to dump our garbage in someone else's backyard.

Come to think of it, recycling just might be the most productive activity in modern America.

David Morris, *St. Paul Pioneer Press*, July 30, 1996.

"A well-run curbside recycling program can cost anywhere from $50 to more than $150 per ton of materials collected. Typical trash collection and disposal programs, on the other hand, cost anywhere from $70 to more than $200 per ton. This demonstrates that, while there's still room for improvements, recycling can be cost-effective."

Opponents of recycling claim that shipping wastes to a landfill is economical. But as of 1995, the costs for landfilling wastes in the United States—not including collection, processing and transport—varied by more than 300 percent, depending on the region and the technology employed at the facility. Thus, it is impossible to claim, as the anti-recycling interests do, that relying on a landfill is—and always will be— the cheapest waste management option.

Far from trashing recycling and impugning the motives of its proponents, all sectors of the polity would do well, materially and spiritually, to embrace and help advance the sustainable, community-building, natural harmony it promotes.

"Recycling can be a conservation triumph, but what makes sense for some materials does not always make sense for others."

Recycling May Not Be the Most Effective Means of Preventing Solid Waste Pollution

Lynn Scarlett

Lynn Scarlett is executive director and a senior fellow of the Reason Public Policy Institute, a nonprofit research organization specializing in environmental policy. In the following viewpoint, she argues that recycling programs cannot be equated with environmental progress because some materials in garbage do not lend themselves to being recycled. Efforts to mandate the use of recycled materials in manufacturing may result in more garbage being produced by stifling innovations in using less materials in making and packaging goods, she concludes.

As you read, consider the following questions:

1. What three things does Scarlett say are required for successful recycling?
2. How has the use of plastic reduced the total volume of garbage being produced, according to the author?
3. What three outcomes does Scarlett believe can result from efforts to mandate more recycling?

Reprinted from Lynn Scarlett, "Recycling Is Politically Correct But Not Always Environmentally Friendly," *San Diego Union-Tribune*, October 6, 1999. Reprinted with permission from the author.

Recycling politics are heating up again. A Georgia-based advocacy group called the Grass Roots Recycling Network is mounting a national campaign—complete with ads in *The New York Times* against a soda maker whose plastic containers fail the group's recycled-content test.

California lawmakers, meanwhile, are wrangling over a bill to mandate increased amounts of recycled content in plastic containers.

Some members of a waste management group allied to the U.S. Conference of Mayors want a German-style program requiring producers to "take back" their packaging and other products after consumers discard them.

These efforts have one thing in common: They all equate recycling with environmental progress. But this focus is too narrow. Some materials are easy to recycle, and some can be composted. But not all.

Sometimes, using recycled content in products can save money, energy and materials. But not always.

Some materials that are hard to recycle or compost are very efficient. They allow companies to make products and packages with very little material and minimal waste.

Waste Reductions

The long-term trend toward less wasteful use of materials is unequivocal. A 1997 report found that consumption of materials per unit of output had dropped by one-third in the United States since 1970. Stoves, water heaters, air conditioners and freezers use less material now than 15 years ago. The weight of packaging for a typical basket of groceries has dropped over 20 percent.

A 1999 report by the U.S. Environmental Protection Agency shows that more efficient use of materials has resulted in waste reductions of over 23 million tons since 1990.

Each package has its own unique tale. Plastic milk jugs and soda bottles are lighter and stronger than 15 years ago.

New materials like flexible plastic packaging used for frozen foods, snack bags and baby diapers have made possible sharp reductions in weight and volume. This is a triumph for conservation.

Recycling can be a conservation triumph, but what makes

sense for some materials does not always make sense for others because of the "Humpty Dumpty problem." Some materials are hard to gather up and reuse.

Successful recycling requires three things.

First, the discards must be easy to isolate from the waste stream. Steel, for example, can be gathered up with powerful magnets.

Second, because recyclables are inputs into new products, the discarded material must be available in uniform quality.

And third, the discards must have "value" in the form of "avoided" manufacturing costs.

Aluminum is a good example of a highly recyclable mate-

How Recycling Causes Environmental Problems

Recycling plants sometimes cause environmental problems, especially in surrounding neighborhoods. Low-income people in southeast Los Angeles, which has dozens of plants, have a particularly hard time understanding recycling's green image.

"There's always glass in the air here," complains Mercedes Arambula, who lives catty-corner from the huge Container Recycling facility on Leota Street in Walnut Park. Huge mounds of broken glass rise to twice the height of an adult in the Container Recycling yard. Skip loaders constantly fill open truck trailers with the glass, which pours down in a dusty stream from the trailers' huge scoops. "I've lived here 18 years," she says. "My kids have asthma now, and my [nephew], who's 1½, is always sick. I won't even let them play in the yard anymore. The trees around my house have all died anyway.". . .

On a local and regional level, recycling is exempted from most regulation, notes Carlos Porras, Southern California Director of Communities for a Better Environment (CBE), because it's viewed as an environmentally positive industry. . . . Recyclers are not required to obtain discharge permits for pollutants; and the air quality management district does not monitor small businesses like recyclers.

"Public policy has allowed recycling plants to crop up without oversight," Porras says. "This is environmental injustice. Regulations are simply not applied to potentially harmful businesses which are located in low-income communities of color, particularly in southeast Los Angeles."

David Bacon, *The Neighborhood Works*, May/June 1998.

rial. Making aluminum requires mining ore, smelting it by using lots of energy, and finally turning it into a usable metal. If all these steps can be circumvented through recycling, the manufacturer saves both materials and energy.

Plastics are the big bugaboo of recycling advocates. Some plastics are recycled, but plastic recycling rates are modest, though not because of a perverse mind-set. It is because of the Humpty Dumpty problem: There are not a lot of "avoided" costs achieved through plastics recycling, especially in some cases.

Plastics are efficient because a wee bit goes a very long way. For example, a tiny wad of shrink wrap clings tightly around a meat tray, replacing much bulkier packaging. This is why plastics are a pre-eminent source-reducing material.

There is another oft-ignored aspect of plastics: The material resulted from an act of recycling! Chemists created plastics by turning waste gases from petroleum refining into polymers, making a barrel of oil almost completely usable.

Yet despite this, recycling advocates are revving up their efforts to force more recycling. These efforts are likely to result in one of three outcomes, none of them good for the environment.

One outcome might be a switch by manufacturers out of plastics. This would erode the benefits that plastics now provide by reducing the bulk and weight of packaging and products.

A second result could be to stifle innovations that use plastics or other new materials.

A third outcome might be Olympian efforts to recycle more plastics, which would be doomed to economic failure and yield dubious environmental benefits.

The Big Picture

No one likes waste, but reducing waste requires understanding the big picture. When manufacturers switch to new materials, it is often because these materials allow them to do more with less: including less energy, less material per unit of product, less transportation fuel, less product breakage.

Ignoring these complexities only deters opportunities for true resource conservation.

> *"Millions each year are afflicted with pollution-induced disease resulting from the use of carbon fuels to produce energy which could be produced by nuclear power."*

Nuclear Energy Is an Environmentally Sound Solution to Preventing Greenhouse Gas Emissions

John Ritch

John Ritch is the U.S. Ambassador to the United Nations Organization in Vienna, Austria, which includes the International Atomic Energy Agency. In the following viewpoint, he contends that nuclear power is the only realistic method by which the growing global demand for energy can be met without releasing greenhouse gases to the world's atmosphere and risking global warming. In addition, he argues that nuclear energy makes much less pollution than the burning of fossil fuels such as coal and oil. He concludes that nuclear energy must be utilized to a greater extent.

As you read, consider the following questions:

1. What three distinct nuclear technologies does Ritch describe?
2. What argument does the author make about the future of renewable energy sources such as solar and wind power?
3. What effects did the Chernobyl accident have on the nuclear power industry, according to Ritch?

Excerpted from John Ritch, "Nuclear Green," *Prospect*, March 1999. Reprinted with permission from *Prospect* magazine, www.prospect-magazine.co.uk.

On the eve of the 21st century, we face an acute green paradox. In the industrial democracies, those most concerned about the potentially cataclysmic effect of pouring billions of tonnes of greenhouse gases into the atmosphere are essentially the same as those most opposed to nuclear energy. In other words, the people who see the global warming problem most vividly are often those most strongly opposed to the most realistic approach to the problem. Similarly, in the developing world, anti-nuclear sentiment appears to be strongest among the forces pressing hardest for democratic reform. Throughout the world (with the notable exception of France) "progressive" politics tends to be "anti-nuclear" politics.

There are understandable historical reasons for this alliance, but it survives in disregard of two profoundly important nuclear success stories. The first is the progress made in establishing an effective regime of non-proliferation of nuclear weapons and in starting to destroy the terrifying nuclear arsenals built up during the cold war. The second is the progress made in making nuclear energy a safe, clean and efficient means of meeting the globe's expanding energy needs—needs which cannot be met by any other non-carbon-based technology, despite the appeal of wind, solar power and other "renewables."

Nuclear Technologies

The word "nuclear" covers three distinct groups of technologies. The first are those required to yield a nuclear explosion. Second are those used to heat water in a reactor, and thereby power an electricity-producing turbine. These technologies have in common the use of uranium and plutonium—fissile material—and the splitting of the atom to release energy. The third group—sometimes called "nuclear applications"—includes technologies which depend on the positive effects of radiation. Although little known to the public, these technologies are dazzling in their diversity and are having a dramatic impact on every aspect of human life. . . .

We have never been in a better position to use nuclear energy safely, and we have never been in greater need of doing so. And yet public understanding of nuclear power remains shrouded in myths and fears quite disproportionate to the facts. My aim is to challenge those myths and offer some facts that bear on future global policy.

Energy Consumption and Global Warming

Today, of the world's 6 billion people, 2 billion have no access to electricity. In the next 25 years, the world's population is expected to grow by 2 billion. We must assume that these 4 billion people—and billions more who today consume very little energy—will exert enormous pressure for higher standards of living and increased global energy consumption. This is a demand we should try to meet, not only to alleviate human misery but also because an increased standard of living is a necessary condition for stabilising the global population. A reasonable prediction is that worldwide energy consumption will increase 50 per cent by the year 2020, and could double by mid-century.

No larger question faces humanity than whether and how this energy demand will be met. Already, at present levels of consumption, we are releasing greenhouse gases—primarily carbon dioxide—at a rate which will cause the total atmospheric accumulation, some time in the 21st century, to almost double from pre-industrial levels.

The greenhouse effect itself is beyond dispute. Indeed, without that capture of heat the surface of the earth would be covered in ice. What remains unknown is what will occur as the greenhouse effect intensifies. But a large majority of scientists predict global warming of several degrees, with catastrophic climatic repercussions. We cannot wait to see. The many-decade lead times involved—the result of the long use of energy infrastructure once built, and the long duration of greenhouse gases once emitted—requires a global energy strategy embodying the principle of "no regrets." Any other policy risks disaster. . . .

Great attention is quite properly focused on energy conservation; this can yield real gains at the margin. But the hopes being attached to renewables—solar and wind power, geothermal energy, biomass and hydroelectric—are quite fantastic in the light of realistic assessments of the role they can play. The potential of the most effective renewable—hydroelectric—has already been heavily exploited and now provides 6 per cent of global energy. But the remaining renewables, which now yield under 1 per cent, offer only limited promise. The World Energy Council predicts that, even with heavy research support and subsidies, these renewables can provide no more than 3–6 per cent of energy supply by 2020. Meanwhile nuclear power, which supplies 6 per cent of global energy (about 17 per cent of global electricity), and remains the one available technology able to meet rising base-load energy needs with negligible greenhouse emissions, is subject to a widespread political taboo.

Even the United Nations (UN) development programme, in its "Energy After Rio" report, dismissed nuclear power as an energy option, citing "public concerns." But political leaders abdicate responsibility if they simply yield to "public concerns" about nuclear power, in attempting to draw up a balanced appraisal of real risks and options. Answering deeply rooted public concerns about nuclear energy means challenging three widespread myths: that nuclear energy fosters nuclear weapons proliferation; that nuclear energy use risks another Chernobyl; and that nuclear waste represents an environmental time bomb.

Nuclear Weapons

The first myth—that nuclear reactors are likely to breed weapons—has little foundation in experience. Each of the five nuclear weapon states built the bomb before moving to civilian power production; technically, power reactors were not a necessary intermediate step.

Furthermore, people seldom recognise our success in controlling nuclear weapons proliferation. The core of all nuclear arms control is the Nuclear Non-Proliferation Treaty (NPT) which, after three decades of diplomacy, is now nearly universal and rigorously enforced. This achievement must be seen against President John F. Kennedy's plausible prediction that our century would see dozens of nations armed with nuclear weapons. Instead, we have capped the number at eight: the five nuclear weapon states on the UN Security Council, who are obliged to engage in good faith disarmament; and the three states—India, Pakistan and Israel—which for their own national security reasons have declined to accept NPT obligations. Apart from these eight countries, every other country in the world is now legally committed—an obligation rigorously overseen by the International Atomic Energy Agency (IAEA)—to abstain from nuclear-weapon development. . . .

Nuclear Accidents

The second myth, which exercises a powerful hold on the public mind, is that a nuclear power plant itself constitutes a kind of bomb—likely, in case of accident, to explode or to release massively fatal doses of radiation. This myth is embodied in collective memory by the accidents at Three Mile Island and Chernobyl. The power of those two images far exceeds what is warranted by the facts.

At Three Mile Island [in Pennsylvania] in 1979, the simple truth is that public health was not endangered. Despite a series of mistakes which seriously damaged the reactor, the only outside effect was an inconsequential release of radiation—negligible when compared to natural radiation in the atmosphere. The citizens of the Three Mile Island area would have received more radiation by taking a flight from New York to Miami or standing for a few minutes amid the granite of Grand Central Station. The protective barriers in the reactor's design worked.

By contrast, the accident at Chernobyl in 1986 [in the former Soviet Union] was a tragedy with serious human and environmental consequences. Chernobyl was a classic product of the Soviet era. A gargantuan reactor lacked the safety technology, the procedures and the protective barriers considered normal elsewhere in the world. The fire led to a massive release of radiation through the open roof of the reactor. More than two dozen firemen died from direct radiation exposure.

A conference sponsored by the World Health Organisation (WHO) on the disaster's tenth anniversary issued a report based on intensive study of the 1.1m[illion] people most directly exposed to the fallout. The main finding was a sharp increase in thyroid cancer among children; 800 cases of the disease had been observed, from which three children had died, with several thousand more cases projected. The report also predicted 3,500 radiation-induced cancer deaths, mainly late in life.

These statistics do not minimise the gravity of what happened at Chernobyl, but they place that singular event in perspective. The nuclear age has now produced more than 8,000 reactor-years of operational time—and one serious accident. Meanwhile, the production and consumption of fossil fuel yields a constant flow of accidents and disease, in addition to greenhouse gases. In the years since Chernobyl, many thousands have died in the production of coal, oil and gas; and millions each year are afflicted with pollution-induced disease resulting from the use of carbon fuels to produce energy which could be produced by nuclear power. According to the WHO, 3m people die each *year* due to air pollution from a global energy system dominated by fossil fuels.

World Nuclear Reactor Construction Starts, 1960–1999

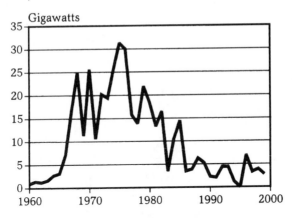

Worldwatch Institute

The question is: what has been done to prevent another Chernobyl? While Chernobyl severely damaged the standing of nuclear power, it inspired important advances in the global industry. Just as [Iraqi leader] Saddam Hussein helped to strengthen safeguards against proliferators, Chernobyl accelerated the arrival of a stronger nuclear safety culture. National regulatory agencies, a new World Association of Nuclear Operators and the IAEA work together to promulgate state-of-the-art knowledge. In 1997, a Convention on Nuclear Safety introduced a system of peer review to detect any deviation from the high safety standards which are now the norm.

For the total of some 440 power reactors (half in Europe) operating in 31 countries, and producing 17 per cent of the world's electricity, only one large safety problem remains: in three countries of the former Soviet empire some 15 plants of the Chernobyl type are still in use. Although now equipped with safety upgrades and better trained personnel, these reactors fall short of current standards and must be phased out as soon as alternative energy supplies can be funded and installed.

Elimination of Chernobyl-style reactors will be an important step in ensuring that the industry will only have reactors of the most modern design. Building on a large base of operating experience, today's reactors are engineered on the principle of "defence in depth," ensuring against a release into the environment even in the case of a severe internal accident. Moreover, designers believe that the newest plants would experience such an environmentally harmless event no more than once in every 100,000 reactor-years of operation. Advanced plants now under development will have even less risk of internal damage.

Nuclear Waste

The fact that modern reactors are immensely safe shifts attention to the question of nuclear waste. The myth is that, regardless of reactor safety, the resulting waste is an insoluble problem—a permanent and accumulating environmental hazard. The reality is that, of all energy forms capable of meeting the world's expanding needs, nuclear power yields the least and most easily managed waste.

The challenge of climate protection arises precisely because it is fossil fuel consumption, not nuclear power, which presents an insoluble waste problem. The problem has two aspects: the huge volume of waste products, primarily gases and particulates; and the method of disposal, which is dispersion into the atmosphere. Neither seems subject to amelioration through technology.

In contrast, nuclear waste is small in volume and subject to sound management. Most nuclear waste consists of relatively short-lived, low and intermediate level waste—annually, some 800 tonnes from an average reactor. Such waste can be handled safely through standard techniques of controlled burial or storage in near-surface facilities. Half of such waste comes from industrial and medical activities rather than from power production.

High level waste consists of spent fuel or the liquid waste which remains after spent fuel is reprocessed to recover uranium or plutonium for further use. The annual global volume of spent fuel from all reactors is 12,000 tonnes. This amount—tiny in comparison to the billions of tonnes of greenhouse gases and many thousands of tonnes of toxic pollutants being discharged annually—can be stored above or below ground. Moreover, the volume decreases considerably if the fuel is reprocessed. The 30 tonnes of spent fuel coming from the average reactor yield a volume of liquid waste of only 10 cubic metres per year.

Even with twice today's number of reactors, the annual global volume of liquid waste, if spent fuel were reprocessed, would be only 9,000 cubic metres—the space occupied by a 2-metre high structure built on a soccer field. Liquid waste from reprocessing can be vitrified into a glass which is chemically stable and subject to a variety of remarkably safe storage techniques. Indeed, the use of those techniques in long-term storage is now more a political than a technical question.

So far, as a result of political obstacles, nations employ various methods of interim storage because no long-term disposal site has been licensed in any country. A number of countries, however, are developing repository concepts. Under consideration are deep underground geological formations such as solid salt domes and granite tunnels which are impervious to water and thus to the leaching of materials. If such sites were used, this protection would be compounded by a series of other barriers: the vitrified state of the waste, high-endurance storage canisters, and a surround of absorbent clayfill. According to the IAEA, even if these barriers were not used, "the long path through the host rock to the surface would probably ensure sufficient dilution so as to pose little risk to human health or the environment." Moreover, storage sites can be designed so that all material remains under strict supervision—and subject to retrieval in the event that technological advance offers new opportunities for retreatment.

Clearly, the management of nuclear waste must meet high standards not only of public safety but also of public acceptance. A first step requires a broader understanding of the waste issue not as a disqualifying liability of the nuclear industry but as a matter of momentous social decision. The choice is between the reckless dispersal of horrendous volumes of fossil fuel emissions and the careful containment of comparatively limited quantities of spent nuclear fuel. To give a stark example: if Europe today were to eliminate nuclear generated electricity and revert to traditional fossil fuel power, the extra greenhouse gases created would be the equivalent of doubling the number of cars on the road.

The Wrong Lesson

For more than 50 years, the words Hiroshima and Nagasaki have served as an unambiguous message of the horror of nuclear war and spurred the world to constructive action. The effect of the word Chernobyl has been more ambiguous. That catastrophe—a singular example of industrial malpractice—could scarcely have been more severe if men had conspired to create the worst debacle in nuclear history. Yet even as scientists and diplomats acted to ensure that such a disaster would never occur again, the word became a rallying cry for resistance to future reliance on nuclear power. This was a lesson wrongly learned.

Today, mankind faces needs, and perils, demanding that we exploit the constructive power of nuclear energy and fulfill President [Dwight] Eisenhower's vision of "Atoms for Peace." Science and diplomacy have paved the way. Politics, and policy, must now follow.

"There is no practical . . . way to eliminate the safety and proliferation threats arising from commercial nuclear power."

Nuclear Energy Is Not an Environmentally Sound Solution to Preventing Greenhouse Gas Emissions

Arjun Makhijani

Nuclear energy is not a good solution to preventing global warming, argues Arjun Makhijani in the following viewpoint. To significantly reduce greenhouse gas emissions would require the construction of thousands of nuclear plants over the next several decades—something he contends is not economically feasible. Nuclear energy plants run the risk of catastrophic accidents such as the 1986 Chernobyl disaster which released radioactive fallout throughout Europe. Nuclear facilities also produce waste which is difficult to store safely, and which could be used to make nuclear weapons. Makhijani is president of the Institute for Energy and Environmental Research, an organization that researches and distributes information on energy and environmental issues to the public.

As you read, consider the following questions:
1. What was the most important lesson of Chernobyl, according to Makhijani?
2. How expensive are nuclear plants to build and operate, according to the author?

Excerpted from Arjun Makhijani, "Nuclear Power: No Solution to Global Climate Change," *Science for Democratic Action*, vol. 6, no. 3, March 1998. Reprinted with permission from the author. Arjun Makhijani holds a Ph.D. from the University of California at Berkeley, where he specialized in controlled nuclear fusion. He has written extensively on energy, nuclear power, nuclear waste, and related issues.

A popular refrain in recent debates on global climate change is that nuclear power must be a significant part of any strategy to reduce greenhouse gas emissions. Proponents argue that, as a carbon-free technology, nuclear power is one of the few ways that carbon dioxide (CO_2) emissions can be significantly reduced while meeting growing energy needs. This claim does not hold up to careful scrutiny, either on technical or economic grounds. Nuclear power and high levels of fossil fuel use each create a diverse set of problems. This viewpoint examines issues relating to nuclear power. . . .

Reactor Safety

There is no practical or reasonable way to eliminate the safety and proliferation threats arising from commercial nuclear power. All reactor types that have been developed or designed pose some level of risk of catastrophic accidents on scales similar to Chernobyl, though the specific accident mechanisms and probabilities depend on reactor design. This is in part because commercial nuclear power was developed as an adjunct to the nuclear arms race and as a tool of Cold War propaganda. In its rush to build new reactors, the industry, from its inception, put public safety, health, environmental protection and even economics behind weapons development and propaganda.

From the early days of reactor development, the Atomic Energy Commission (AEC) was aware of the possibility for catastrophic accidents. In 1957, Brookhaven National Laboratory published an assessment, known by its report number, WASH-740, which outlined the potential health and property damages that could result from a severe reactor accident. Several months after the release of the report, Congress passed the Price-Anderson Act, limiting liability of utilities to $500 million—just ten percent of the property damage costs estimated in WASH-740. This amount was increased to $7 billion in 1988, still far below the likely damages of such an accident.

The nuclear industry continues to downplay the potential for catastrophic reactor accidents, despite the evidence presented by the Chernobyl disaster in April, 1986. The explosion and fire at Chernobyl deposited fallout on every country in the northern hemisphere and forced the evacuation of over 100,000 people in a 30 kilometer zone around the plant, and the abandonment of 250,000 to 375,000 acres of agricultural land. But the nuclear industry as well as the International Atomic Energy Agency (IAEA), citing erroneous official Soviet data and ignoring the lack of accurate data on health effects, have tended to minimize the significance of the accident. Official estimates of the radioactivity released in the first ten days were 80 million curies. But in an independent assessment, Soviet scientist Zhores Medvedev estimated that the releases of radioiodine and radiocesium were about three times higher than officially stated. The overall costs of Chernobyl are difficult to calculate, but even the official estimates of about ten to fifteen billion dollars surpass the $7 billion liability limit of the Price-Anderson Act.

The most important and tragic lesson of Chernobyl is that the most severe kind of nuclear power accident can actually happen. Moreover, the problems created by such severe accidents will persist for many generations. While claims have been made for a new generation of "inherently safe reactors," they are exaggerated and highly misleading. It would take many decades to test various designs to determine whether creating a practical reactor that is economical and invulnerable to catastrophic accidents is achievable at all. Consequently, nuclear power cannot safely help the world reduce carbon dioxide emissions—a pressing need that must be addressed with policies in place in the next few years. . . .

Economics

Nuclear power is a far more expensive and risky way of generating electricity than highly efficient combined cycle natural gas plants. Even in France, which is highly dependent on nuclear power, officials have admitted that combined cycle electricity plants using natural gas are more economical than nuclear power plants. Each nuclear plant built can typically be expected to cost from about $1 billion to several billion dollars in excess lifetime costs. To make a substantial reduction in CO_2 emissions, nuclear power plants would not only have to supply much of the world's electricity growth but also replace many coal-fired plants as they are retired.

This would require the construction of on the order of 2,000 nuclear power plants (1,000 megawatts (MW) each) in the next several decades. The total cost penalty of using nuclear would amount to several trillion dollars. This vast sum of money would have to come in the form of subsidies from governments and/or electricity ratepayers (in the form of higher prices). It could be much more efficiently used to make investments in energy efficiency, cogeneration, renewables, combined-cycle power plants, fuel cells and the like. Thus, investments in nuclear power will detract from efforts to reduce carbon dioxide emissions by preempting more appropriate investments. . . .

Disarmament Issues

The challenges of non-proliferation and disarmament issues are even more daunting and basic than safety and economic issues, because they are not only technological, but also military, political, and institutional in nature.

Plutonium is made in all commercial reactors. Once separated by reprocessing, the plutonium in this spent fuel can be used to make nuclear weapons. Stocks of separated commercial plutonium have been growing very rapidly since the early 1980s and are set to surpass military stocks in the next few years. . . .

If nuclear power were used as a means of reducing greenhouse gas emissions, the inventories of plutonium would rise dramatically. If 2,000 new nuclear power plants are built over the next several decades (in addition to replacing the present 350,000 MW of nuclear capacity), the global inventory of commercial plutonium would rise to about 20,000 metric tons by the middle of the next century, dwarfing present stocks. This inventory, the pressure on uranium resources, and the popular opposition to nuclear waste repositories would greatly intensify pressures for commercial plutonium separation and the use of such plutonium in nuclear reactors. This would further exacerbate economic, environmental, and proliferation problems associated with nuclear power.

Nuclear technology has been glamorized as "high technology" for decades, and its promotion is part of the Nuclear

Non-Proliferation Treaty. Western propaganda dates back at least to President Dwight Eisenhower's December 1953 "Atoms for Peace" speech, in which he connected renunciation of nuclear weapons to the promotion of nuclear energy. The result of these Cold War policies is huge governmental or subsidized private establishments in key countries with a vested interest in plutonium economies. These bureaucracies continue to be politically and financially powerful despite the environmental, non-proliferation, and economic failures of key technologies such as breeder reactors and reprocessing. . . .

Radioactive Waste

As discussed above, for nuclear power to contribute significantly to the reduction of greenhouse gases, thousands of new nuclear power plants would be needed. This would result in the creation of hundreds of thousands of metric tons of spent fuel in addition to existing wastes. There is no viable policy for the management of spent fuel at the present time. Nuclear power advocates see the "solution" of building a geologic repository as an essential element in the revival of nuclear power, at least in the United States. This has evoked the counter response of opposition to repositories until the issue of long-term management can be separated from promotion of nuclear power. Proposals to manage the waste through transmutation (changing long-lived radioactive elements into short-lived ones), are not viable for several reasons. Transmutation will not only require nuclear reactors of one sort or another; it will require implementation of reprocessing technologies that can also be modified for production of weapons-usable materials. Transmutation and reprocessing technologies will also create their own waste management problems by generating large new volumes of radioactive waste. Thus, what appears at first to be a technical answer to the problem of proliferation and waste management is likely to exacerbate proliferation problems without really solving waste management problems. Besides failing to eliminate the need for repositories or other disposal strategies, these technologies remain very expensive, and would greatly increase the cost of nuclear power, which is already uncompetitive.

Phasing Out Nuclear Power

In addition to the safety, proliferation, and economic drawbacks cited above, there are a number of reasons why a nuclear phase-out is necessary to a sustainable, peaceful and healthy energy future, including:

- The presence of large stocks of separated plutonium as well as plutonium in spent fuel can make reversion to a nuclear armed state in times of tension and war more likely.
- The bureaucracies that are most eager to promote nuclear power are also the ones that tend to promote nuclear weapons in many countries, including the present nuclear weapons states. These nuclear bureaucracies continue to harbor hopes of a plutonium economy despite the technological, environmental, and economic failures of nuclear power. This is a continuing incitement to proliferation, declaratory policy notwithstanding.
- Nuclear power plants can become targets in conventional wars, greatly increasing environmental and health devastation. . . .

Unless the West, which first glamorized nuclear power, renounces it and begins to phase it out, others are unlikely to give it up. Nor will the West have a basis to deny this technology to others. . . . While a phase-out of nuclear power in the West does not guarantee progress on other issues or, for that matter, a phase out in all other countries, it is an essential condition for making problems associated with oil, natural gas, and greenhouse gas build-up more manageable.

Periodical Bibliography

The following articles have been selected to supplement the diverse views presented in this chapter. Addresses are provided for periodicals not indexed in the *Readers' Guide to Periodical Literature*, the *Alternative Press Index*, the *Social Sciences Index*, or the *Index to Legal Periodicals and Books*.

Robert W. Crandall — "The Costly Pursuit of the Impossible," *Brookings Review*, Summer 1997.

Brian Doherty — "Selling Air Pollution," *Reason*, 1996.

Scott Farrow and Michael A. Toman — "Using Benefit-Cost Analysis to Improve Environmental Regulations," *Environment*, March 1999.

Fred Friedman — "Creating Markets for Recycling," *Dollars and Sense*, July/August 1999.

White Gibons — "Whither Our Air and Water?" *World & I*, June 1999. Available from 3400 New York Ave. NE, Washington, DC 20078-0760.

Ted Halstead — "Why Tax Work?" *Nation*, April 20, 1998.

Jeremy B. Hockenstein et al. — "Crafting the Next Generation of Market-Based Environmental Tools," *Environment*, May 1997.

Loren McArthur and Marc Breslow — "Polluters and Politics," *Dollars and Sense*, July/August 1998.

Arthur H. Purcell — "Trash Troubles," *World & I*, November 1998. Available from 3400 New York Ave. NE, Washington, DC 20078-0760.

Richard Rhodes and Denis Beller — "The Need for Nuclear Power," *Foreign Affairs*, January/February 2000.

Dawn Stover — "The Nuclear Legacy," *Popular Science*, August 1995.

John Tierney — "Recycling Is Garbage," *New York Times Magazine*, June 30, 1996.

Brian Tokar — "Trading Away the Earth," *Dollars and Sense*, March/April 1996.

Clark Wiseman — "Recycling Revisited," *PERC Reports*, August 1997. Available from 502 S. 19th Ave., Suite 211, Bozeman, MT 59718.

CHAPTER 3

Is the American Lifestyle Bad for the Environment?

Chapter Preface

The personal automobile is a central component of life for most Americans. The majority of Americans rely on their cars to get from their homes to workplaces, schools, stores, and other destinations. There is evidence that this dependence is growing. For example, the total miles Americans traveled in their cars grew by more than 40 percent between 1983 and 1990.

The popularity of cars carries a cost, however. Many environmentalists have argued that automobiles cause significant damage to the environment. Automobiles create air pollution, including greenhouse gas emissions that may contribute to global warning. They also leave behind toxins and chemicals such as petroleum residues on roads, which run off and contaminate groundwater. The increasing number of cars requires the construction of paved roads and parking lots, resulting in the loss of wild habitats and other open spaces. On the global scale, many worry about what might happen if people in developing nations succeed in emulating the American lifestyle, including ownership of cars. "If the Chinese began driving at the same rate as Americans," writes Charles Komanoff, "they would increase the world's emissions of carbon dioxide . . . by 25 percent."

Does preserving the environment mean that Americans must give up their cars and rely on bicycles and mass transit? While some automobile critics see this as a reasonable goal, others have proposed less drastic measures. Some encourage carpooling, while others call for automobile makers to use technology to make cars more efficient and less polluting. Others argue for changes in how cities and suburbs are developed in order to reduce dependence on cars. The automobile is one example of how environmental problems cannot be blamed solely on the actions of manufacturers, but result from the everyday actions of people. The viewpoints in this chapter examine the environmental impact of automobiles and other aspects of the American lifestyle.

"Our pro-fossil fuel government and industry underwrite the car culture that undermines planet preservation."

Automobile Use in America Must Be Discouraged to Save the Environment

Jane Holtz Kay

The automobile is an integral part of the lives of most Americans. In the following viewpoint, Jane Holtz Kay argues that extensive automobile use has led to significant environmental problems such as air pollution, global warming, and the disappearance of open space to suburban sprawl. America's dependence on the automobile is fostered in part by government policies that subsidize automobile use and fail to account for the automobile's social and environmental costs. She calls for raising taxes on gasoline, investing in public transportation, and reforming land use policies to discourage the use of cars. Kay is the author of *Asphalt Nation: How the Automobile Took Over America and How We Can Take It Back.*

As you read, consider the following questions:
1. How much fuel and pollution do cars in America consume and produce every second, according to Kay?
2. What is the total of the "hidden costs" cars incur to society, according to the author?
3. What should the price of gasoline be raised to, according to Kay?

Reprinted from Jane Holtz Kay, "Infernal Combustion," *In These Times*, August 8, 1999. Reprinted with permission from *In These Times*.

You don't need a weatherman to tell you that the whole earth has become the scorched earth. And you don't need a climate course to teach you that the temperature has become hot news. In the hottest decade of the millennium, "severe weather alerts" are as constant as the calendar.

It started last winter [of 1998] with the headlines: "South Gets White Christmas and Loses Power" and "California Farmers Hope to Salvage Some Citrus." It continued with blizzards in the Midwest, tornados in Florida, and hot-to-warm climate quick steps in New England. By late spring [of 1999], the Los Angeles cool and the East Coast steam had reversed the natural order of the continent.

But if weather scares have chilled us out and heated our consciousness, there is one thing that the fluctuating thermometer and rising tides don't record. And that's the complicity of the car. Whatever the assessment of the damage of the capricious climate, the political and financial barometers have yet to register the largest single contributor to global warming.

"Is your current car too closely related to the fossil fuel it burns?" asks an advertisement for a luxury automobile. You bet it is. Our stock of motor vehicles is not only related to rising temperatures and erratic weather but a parent of the problem. In just one example, the Atmosphere Alliance has blamed a sharp jump of 3.4 percent in U.S. emission—more than the total of most nations—on one automoted energy hog, the sport-utility vehicle.

But SUVs on steroids are just the newest phase of U.S. auto-dependency. Clock the minutes: Every second the nation's 200 million motor vehicles travel 60,000 miles, use 3,000 gallons of petroleum products and add 60,000 pounds of carbon dioxide to the atmosphere—that's two-thirds of U.S. carbon dioxide emissions.

A Dirty Secret

The surprise is that despite the motor vehicle's role in making the weather gyrate like a Dow Jones graph, the total cost of America's auto-dependency remains a dirty but hidden secret. The roads we build to serve the car, the fuel we extract, the industrial energy consumed in producing 15 million motor vehicles a year are enormous—and largely unrecorded. U.S. cars and trucks carry three-quarters of a trillion dollars in hidden costs. Often lacking a dollar sign, their tally ranges from parking facilities to police protection; from registry operations to uncompensated accidents. Cars bought on the installment plan drive up consumer debt by 40 percent, making the General Motors Acceptance Corporation the largest consumer finance institution in the world. And we haven't even calculated the environmental cost of global warming in repairing the damage from floods and fires.

How do we right this equation? We need to acknowledge the exactions of our auto-based existence. The love affair with the motor vehicle that festoons our policy like a GM hood ornament comes at a steep price, personally, socially and environmentally.

Beyond the $93 billion a year that local, state and national governments spend on roads, we must tally other expenditures, from the 41,500 lives lost annually in car accidents to the automobiles and auto parts that account for two-thirds of our trade deficit with Japan. From 8 billion hours a year stuck in traffic to the $100 billion a year spent on the military budget defending our Middle East oil supply, the visible and invisible costs of the car mount. Count, too, the rising cost of that oil extraction as we labor to clean or discover new reserves, which are predicted to dwindle and become pricier on their way to exhaustion.

Costs of Sprawl

Beyond building and running our cars, there is the environmental and financial toll of car-bred sprawl. The land bulldozed into asphalt is a lost opportunity cost. The wetlands and farmland paved (2 million arable acres a year), the open space or city split by an arterial highway, or the hilltop sprouting the four-leaf clover interstate is, to say the least, a minus.

Then there are the other invisible losses. The price of car-bred infrastructure subsidized to take us to the sprawling edges demands, in turn, an evermore pricey and energy-squandering infrastructure of electricity, cable and sewage lines at the end of the road. Consider that by laying asphalt for the automobile, we give over more than half our cities to roads and parking lots. (Note how each automobile demands seven spaces to move and park—one at home, one at work, one at the mall and four for the road network.) Chart our subsidies for such incidentals as parking: for one, the 85 million employees given free spaces whose real estate is worth an average of $1,000 apiece. This amounts to an $85 billion lure—and $85 billion denied to non-drivers. No other country carries our loss in property taxes from such "investments." Finally, compute the price of 4,000 "dead" malls and countless Main Streets languishing in the wake of the highway-based exodus. The tragic loss of community cannot be reckoned.

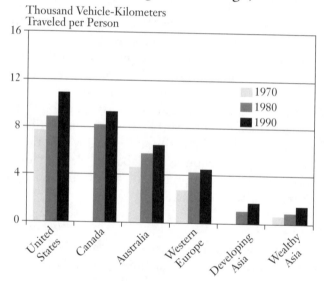

Annual per Capita Car Use in Selected World Cities, by Regional Average, 1970–90

Worldwatch Institute, *Vital Signs 1999.*

What false economy allows us to dismiss these debts? To simply credit highway-based transportation as 18 percent of our gross domestic product—more than health and education combined? What perverse sense of the environmental balance sheet lets us tamper with the fate of the planet without noting these debts? In the end, our pro-fossil fuel government and industry underwrite the car culture that undermines planet preservation. It favors the private car vs. public transportation at seven-to-one, offers single-family mortgages and policies that undercut core cities and suburbs, and gives the highway men a free lunch on a silver platter.

Policy Recommendations

Curbing the car to protect the climate is good financial as well as environmental policy. Making the car pay its way by altering pricing policies to stop the subsidies would reduce costs while cutting fossil fuel. Raising the tax on gas—or on carbon dioxide–spewing gas guzzlers or on number of miles driven—would lessen auto use and impact. So would congestion pricing, tolls and parking fees. It is time to follow the other industrialized nations of the world by raising gas prices to $4 or $5 a gallon, funnelling these funds to good public transportation and lessening the need for autos in the first place.

Changing sprawl-inducing land patterns that have made two or three cars a (perceived) prerequisite in half our households is also essential. By reinvesting in public transportation, good planning, mixed-use zoning and other improved land use policies, we create dense neighborhoods and urban infill for the clustered physical environment that supports the mass transit, trains, bicycling and walking that will ease us out of the car trap.

None of these routes to reduce auto-dependency and halt global warming is built in a day, but they can begin instantly on a personal and political level. As Washington and Wall Street slouch their way to climate protection, we need to do more—far more—than give lip service to this mindset. "Cogito Ergo Zoom" is how *Automobile* magazine describes America's attitude to the internal combustion machine. More cogitating and less zoom would be better. So would activism from the bottom and leadership from the top to replace a mentality as stuck in traffic as our way of life. The Atlantic would be rolling across the Adirondacks and the glaciers melting into Miami before the people who brought us the *Exxon Valdez* and the Corvair flipped the switch on their course to stop climatic upheaval. It is time for the rest of us to brake the automotive gluttons that fuel global disarray.

"At the highest levels of government, . . . there has been and continues to be a war on drivers."

A War on Automobiles to Save the Environment Is Not Justified

Alan Caruba

For the past several decades, the federal government and the international environmental movement has waged a campaign to discourage automobile use and even rid America of automobiles, claims Alan Caruba in the following viewpoint. Such a campaign cannot be justified on environmental grounds, he argues. Improving technologies have made automobiles far more efficient and less polluting than in the past. Americans, he asserts, should not be coerced into giving up their cars. Caruba is the founder of the National Anxiety Center, a clearinghouse for information on environmentalism and other issues.

As you read, consider the following questions:
1. What kinds of regulations have been imposed on car drivers, according to Caruba?
2. What is the fundamental goal of the worldwide environment movement, according to the author?
3. What contention does the author make about global warming?

Reprinted from Alan Caruba, "The War on Drivers," 1998. Reprinted with permission from The National Anxiety Center. Article available at www.anxietycenter.com.

Like most Americans, I had always been vaguely aware that the cost of owning a car, buying a new one, and the general use of cars nationwide, had been rising for years. There were, in addition, new obstacles and restrictions being imposed.

This became evident once again in December 1998 when the Environmental Protection Agency (EPA) began to institute hefty fines on owners of the nation's gasoline stations and others who store fuel, as The New York Times reported, "in potentially leaky underground tanks . . ." The key word here is "potentially." According to the EPA, an estimated 400,000 tanks, which may or may not be leaking anything, remain after that agency had taken action to either ban the use or require the replacement of some 600,000 tanks.

The significance of this for drivers is that an estimated 70,000 gasoline stations are still deemed out of compliance, something that can cost between $100,000 and $200,000 to achieve. Many small communities throughout the nation will simply lose access to their only gasoline station. Already across the nation, many dealers have elected to stop providing gas and depend solely on auto repair for income. For countless Americans, particularly in rural areas, filling up is going to become a major problem.

Over the years, motorists have had to accept traffic that slows to a crawl thanks to high occupancy vehicle (HOV) lanes and even mandatory car-pooling regulations. These costs and annoyances had crept up on all Americans in incremental stages, each seeming to come from the need to "clean up the air", "become more energy efficient", and "increase the use of mass transit."

It didn't seem to matter that, preceding and during the decades this was occurring, the movement of people and businesses to the suburbs had increased dramatically or that, for most people, average commuting time to work by car was barely ten to twenty minutes. It didn't matter that most suburban-based moms spent most of their trips chauffering their children or husbands around. Work commutes for women, for example, constitute only 18%, dwarfed by personal trips at 46%, necessitated by day-care, school, going to the market or dry cleaners, and other everyday tasks.

It didn't seem to matter that, by 1998, most major cities such as Cleveland, Boston, and Chicago, had achieved the biggest percentage drop in average days per year that violated federal air standards. The air *is* getting cleaner.

A War on Drivers

Slowly, I became aware of a *virtual war on drivers (and truckers)* being orchestrated by the Federal government which, in turn, imposed mandates upon the States.

Then, while reading Al Gore, Jr's book, *Earth In The Balance*, I became aware of the astonishing agenda behind the problems drivers were incurring. He wrote that "it ought to be possible to establish a coordinated global program to accomplish the strategic goal of *completely eliminating the internal combustion engine over, say, a twenty-five year period.*" (Emphasis added) Or, to put it another way, by the year 2018!

"We now know," Gore wrote of cars and trucks, "*that their cumulative impact on the global environment is posing a mortal threat to the security of every nation we are ever again likely to confront.*" (Emphasis added) This is nuts!

Gore, however, was simply putting in print one of the most fundamental goals of the worldwide environmental movement which, in the United States, gained governmental status when the EPA was established in 1970 and, worldwide, through the granting of "Non-Governmental Organization" status by the United Nations to countless environmental organizations. They, in turn, literally create international policy through UN-sponsored treaties such as the Kyoto treaty on climate control which would impose huge energy use restrictions on the U.S. while exempting nations such as China and India.

Unnecessary Regulations

Consider what occurred under the Clinton-Gore administration. Despite the fact that the air has been showing extraordinary improvements since the 1970's laws went into effect, the EPA actually imposed *tighter rules for emissions* of "smog causing gases and soot from cars and light trucks beginning in 2004," as reported in April 1998 by the *New York Times*.

But why? Eric Peters, an authority on transportation issues, in a December 22, 1998 article that appeared in the *Washington Times*, pointed out that, "Since at least the mid-1980's, new cars and trucks have been equipped with an impressive array of computer-controlled anti-pollution hardware that is largely self-policing," adding that "current model year cars and trucks are equipped with systems that surpass the computer power of the Lunar Module."

Despite this, state by state, car and truck owners must submit to intensive inspections which literally test themselves every time the ignition key is turned! Moreover, *less than five percent (5%) of all currently registered vehicles are cars older than model year 1980*. Those older cars, even if they did pollute, would contribute an infinitesimal amount.

Demonizing Sport Utility Vehicles

The media attention given SUVs may be only an advance wave of a major push to demonize larger vehicles. As early as 1997, network TV featured a news story reporting increasing nationwide prices for gasoline. The suggestion was inserted that the blame should be placed on people who drive larger, "gas-guzzling" vehicles. By early 1998, government reports were listing SUVs in order of "aggressiveness," as if the vehicles themselves were somehow responsible for causing accidents and injuring people.

Does this sound familiar? It should to most gunowners. The same techniques of vilifying mechanical objects were used before each big push for more gun controls.

Hunters and shooters already know there is an unrelenting pressure group that doesn't like guns and would like to take them away. Guess what? They don't like your vehicles either.

John Malloy, *Gun News Digest*, Spring 1999.

Ironically, the catalytic converter, an invention that has sharply reduced smog caused by auto emissions, was deemed "a growing cause of global warming" by the EPA, according to a *New York Times* article in April 1998! The article reported that, "This spring, the EPA published a study estimating that nitrous oxide now accounts for about 7.2 percent of the gases that cause global warming." Unreported, as is always the case with the *New York Times*, was the fact that *there is no global warming*. The earth hasn't warmed at all for the past fifty years. The global warming theory was discredited in 1998 by the man who first introduced it to Congress in 1988.

In short, it doesn't matter how energy efficient and non-polluting cars are or will be, the EPA quite simply will always raise the bar, even if means condemning the very technology that makes cars operate to produce cleaner emissions.

More ominous, because the vast bulk of all goods manufactured and sold in the U.S. is moved by truck, was the EPA announcement, also in April 1998, that "exhaust from the (diesel) engines probably causes cancer in humans." The feds are now gearing up to include the nation's trucking system in its war on drivers. This is madness.

It doesn't end there. By the summer of 1998, the National Highway Traffic Safety Administration was advocating *replacing all light trucks, i.e. pickups, minivans, and sport-utility vehicles*, with cars because it would, they said, save 2,000 lives each year. More people drown each year just taking a swim. The NHTSA had earlier proposed putting safety belts and other devices on golf cars! The lunatics are running the asylum!

What *really* is happening on our highways and roads? Well, in 1997, *the death rate on the nation's roads fell to a record low.* The U.S. Department of Transportation concluded there were 1.6 deaths per 100 million miles traveled. Mind you, this occurred despite efforts to get Americans to use trains and other mass transit. For example, the future of Amtrak [the government-run passenger railway system] is even more shaky. Since its inception in 1970, the number of miles traveled by car has risen by two thirds to more than *2.6 trillion.*

In December 1998, New Jersey Governor Christie Whitman publicly celebrated the end of a long fight with the EPA which ended the imposition of HOV lanes on two major thoroughfares. The state's largest circulation newspaper, which had championed an end to the HOV's, reported that "traffic was moving better on Route 80 than it has in years. Same for most of Route 287." This in a state with the highest population density in the nation and where more cars are owned than there are people.

The EPA's coercive threat to deny New Jersey taxpayers their own money to improve their own highway system had been thwarted. Now, we have to do this in every state in the Union. And we have until 2004 to rescind the new EPA clean air restrictions.

Federal Government's Lies

We need to understand that the air *is* getting cleaner, that cars not only pollute far less, but monitor their own emissions, that raising speed limits has not led to more deaths, that just about everything the EPA and other federal agencies have been telling us is a lie.

Mostly, however, we have to understand that, at the highest levels of government, aided and abetted by the worldwide environmental movement, there has been and continues to be a war on drivers.

"The ecological demands of average citizens in wealthy countries exceed global per capital supply of resources by a factor of nearly three."

American Wealth and Consumption Patterns Degrade the Environment

David Schaller

Every living person makes an "ecological footprint" on the environment through consuming resources and discarding waste, writes David Schaller in the following viewpoint. Schaller briefly examines this concept and writes that people in America and other developed nations have a much larger impact on the environment than people in developing nations such as India. Responsibility for global environmental problems lies more with the consumption patterns of rich nations rather than population growth in poor nations, he concludes. Schaller is a sustainable development expert with the Denver (Colorado) Regional Office of the Environmental Protection Agency.

As you read, consider the following questions:
1. How does Schaller define "ecological footprint"?
2. How many acres of productive land are needed to support the average North American lifestyle, according to Schaller?
3. What big question exists over resource use and waste elimination technologies, according to the author?

Reprinted from David Schaller, "Our Footprints Are All Over the Place," *Regulatory Intelligence Data*, February 5, 1999.

The word "footprint" offers us many richly symbolic images: Neil Armstrong's "one small step"; Crusoe's Friday; Sandburg's fog that comes "on little cat feet"; the [fossilized] Olduvai tracks of Australopithecus; and yes, even the caution expressed by my elementary school teacher to stay away from "Big Feet"—the junior high kids on the playground who loved to torment first- and second-graders.

Let's consider another type of footprint, one equally symbolic and full of meaning to those concerned about environmental protection.

If asked who had the bigger "footprint"—an adult female living somewhere in the developing world or your average eight-year-old American child—most would select the adult female. Now, insert the word "ecological" in front of "footprint" and repeat the question. The answer may surprise.

Ecological Footprints

The concept of an "ecological footprint" turns out to be an almost intuitive measure of the impact of individuals or societies on nature. It provides a simple yet elegant accounting tool that can help us see the impact of human consumption patterns on the earth. What we do about this information, of course, is the essence of a much larger policy debate.

As we live out our lives, we consume resources and discard wastes. Each bit of consumption and generation of waste demands a certain amount of productive land and water. The amount of productive land and water needed to support the production of resources we consume and absorb the wastes we create can be considered our ecological footprint.

Individuals, households, cities, regions, nations—all can be measured as to their ecological footprint.

In their compelling book, *Our Ecological Footprint*, William Rees and Mathis Wackernagel lay out the approach that is changing the way many look at broad issues of sustainability, ecological carrying capacity, environmental protection, and even social justice. The authors take us through the number crunching and data sources used to calculate footprints for us, our cities, and our nations. For Western societies, the findings are less than comforting.

A Global Analysis

Here, in a nutshell, is "footprint" analysis applied to the world in which we live:

The ecologically productive land of the world now totals some 3.6 acres for each of the 5.9 billion people now alive. The average North American lifestyle requires almost 10 acres of ecologically productive lands to supply its resources and absorb its wastes. Thus, the ecological demands of average citizens in wealthy countries exceed global per capita supply of resources by a factor of nearly three. Someone, lots of someones, somewhere are going without.

Ten Billion Tons

Imagine a truck delivering to your house each morning all the materials you use in a day, except food and fuel. Piled at the front door are the wood in your newspaper, the chemicals in your shampoo, and the plastic in your grocery bags. Metal in your appliances and your car—just that day's share of those items' total lives—are also included, as is your daily fraction of shared materials, such as the stone and gravel in your office walls and in the streets you stroll. At the base of the pile are materials you never see, including the nitrogen and potash used to grow your food, and the earth and rock under which your metals and minerals were once buried.

If you are an average American, this daily delivery would be a burdensome load: at 101 kilos, it is roughly the weight of a large man. But your materials tally has only begun. Tomorrow, another 101 kilos arrive, and the next day, another. By month's end, you have used three tons of material, and over the year, 37 tons. And your 270 million compatriots are doing the same thing, day in and day out. Together, you will consume nearly 10 billion tons of material in a year's time.

Gary Gardner and Payal Sompat, *Mind Over Matter: Recasting the Role of Materials in Our Lives*, Worldwatch Paper 144, December 1998.

Said another way, if everyone currently alive were to consume resources and generate wastes at the pace of the average citizen in the U.S. (or Canada, or western Europe, or Japan) we would need three planets of ecologically productive lands.

This projection assumes that there will be no improvements in either resource use efficiency or waste elimination techniques. However, we know that improvements in both are happening. The big question is whether they are happening fast enough.

It is, of course, in the inefficiency of resource production that wastes are created, our "environmental" problems manifested, and the Environmental Protection Agency's mission defined. But if we are not looking hard at how and where our "footprint" is placed, we are missing the chance to do something about those inefficiencies.

When we use the ecological footprint concept to measure the resource use and waste generation of the average North American, it becomes clear that via trade and technology we have "appropriated" the ecological capacity of large areas outside our own national boundaries. We have, in fact, exported much of our "footprint." Responsibility for a good deal of the world's environmental problems starts to hit home.

Policy Implications

So where do we go with this? Some would prefer to start with that hypothetical adult female in the developing world whose fecundity promises to add billions more footprints to the earth's surface in the coming decades. The accounting tool of ecological footprints suggests, however, that the place to begin is with the resource consuming, waste generating "average" inhabitant of North America, western Europe, and Japan.

Limiting the number of poor people in distant countries may make for popular policy, but it does little about the root cause of our environmental and related socio-economic problems. The two ounces of rice that a billion of our poorest neighbors call their "daily bread" leaves a rather transparent ecological footprint. Those one billion could "go away" tomorrow, and our global ecological unraveling would go on unabated.

The answer to our earlier question? It is the eight-year-old child (not to mention his parents, neighbors, and friends) who now has the "Big Feet."

"It is the rich who can cherish the wilderness because they no longer have to choose between their own survival and nature's."

American Wealth and Consumption Patterns Enhance the Environment

Peter Huber

It is not wealth, but poverty, that is the main engine of environmental degradation, argues Peter Huber in the following viewpoint. America and other wealthy nations have the capital and knowledge to use resources efficiently, and its citizens are wealthy enough to demand environmental protections. Poor nations, he asserts, produce more pollution and use up more land because they waste resources and are more concerned with everyday survival than with the environment. Huber is a research fellow at the Manhattan Institute for Policy Research, a columnist for *Forbes* magazine, and author of *Hard Green: Saving the Environment from the Environmentalists.*

As you read, consider the following questions:

1. Why have forests in the North American continent been expanding since around 1920, according to Huber?
2. Why are poor countries bad at practicing conservation, according to the author?
3. What connection does Huber make between wealth and population?

Reprinted from Peter Huber, "Wealth Is Green," March 23, 2000. Reprinted with permission from IntellectualCapital.com. Available at www.IntellectualCapital.com.

The rich are ruining the planet. A mere 5% of the world's population lives in the United States, but Americans consume 20% to 40% of "resources"—fossil fuels, electricity, copper, aluminum, zinc and so forth. If the rest of the world lived as we do, it would take "two planet earths" to feed and fuel it. Or so we are often told. But the facts—the important ones—show otherwise.

The Difference Between Rich and Poor

Our pioneer ancestors leveled some 200 million acres of North American forest for farmland and pasture. Since 1920, however, we have been reforesting the continent. For at least a century, now, the average American has eaten more food, and consumed more energy, even as the American farmer has plowed fewer acres and harvested less wood. The result has been an extraordinary environmental renaissance on our continent.

What happened? Quite simply, we learned to live in three dimensions, not just two. We learned to draw less of our wealth from the living surface of the planet, and more from its sterile depths. Cement, steel and synthetic plastics displaced hardwoods in our ships, dwellings and furniture, leaving the wood itself to the forest. Fossil and nuclear fuels displaced wood in our residential and industrial furnaces. Fertilizers, pesticides, factory farms and high-yield crops from the laboratory substituted, at the margin, for some three-quarters of the acres once needed to produce equivalent amounts of food. By extending human enterprise into the third dimension, we have painlessly retreated from the two-dimensional surface, where the rest of life dwells.

Poor countries are horribly bad at conservation because they lack the capital and know-how that we have put to such good use. For the poor, the elephant remains a mountain of meat, the whale is a barrel of oil, and the rain forest is a place to grow cassava, once the monkeys have been shot and the undergrowth cleared by fire. Despite their small appetites, developing-world countries manage to generate a lot of garbage, smoke and trash. They consume little, but they are wasteful and destructive. They use no pesticide and plow more land; they use no plastics and discard far more organic waste; they eat little meat and shoot more elephants.

Capital and Knowledge

Moving our Western economy into the third dimension has required one input above all others: capital. It takes vast amounts of it to extract oil from two miles beneath Alaskan ice or Saudi sand, or to process the oil into plastics that then displace teak and ivory, or to reconfigure the genes that quadruple yields on the farm. From wood to coal to oil to uranium, the higher the technology the more capital it requires to burn it, and the less natural resource.

The second crucial input to the three-dimensional economy has been knowledge. The mystery is not why we consume so many resources so fast—from so deep in the earth—it is why thousands of generations of shivering, starving humanity left so much wealth untouched. And it is not much of a mystery, at that. Oil two miles beneath Alaskan ice or Saudi sand is not "wealth" at all. It does not belong to anyone, least of all to "the world." We call such things "resources" by convention, but the "resource" is not the stuff itself; it is knowing how to get it. Anyone can gather wood and burn it—man has been doing that successfully for tens of thousands of years. Gathering and burning uranium is much harder, but a tiny volume of it, prepared just so, can heat and light an entire city.

The happier Third World economies today are what ours were 50 years ago; the unhappier ones are what ours were some centuries earlier. Why should we expect them to be green? We weren't when we were as poor as they are. Victorian England is not a shining example of environmental rectitude for modern London. Buffalo Bill was not a paladin of wise husbandry on the American range. We have no reason to be proud of our own environmental past—which is, by and large, the Third World's environmental present.

Population Growth and Wealth

Finally, it is wealth—not poverty—that is now ending the sprawl of humanity itself. Developed-world fertility has been falling quite steadily for two centuries. In the United States, it dropped from eight children per woman to two. In what the United Nations calls the "more developed regions," the "total fertility rate" (roughly speaking, the average number of children born per woman) has fallen from 2.8 children per woman in the 1950–55 time frame to 1.6 today. That puts it well below the replacement rate. Exactly the same is now happening in developing countries as they grow wealthier. The fertility rate in India today is lower than the American rate in the 1950s. Fertility rates in most sub-Saharan African nations are falling steadily.

Wealth and the Environment

In the early part of [the twentieth] century the United States was much poorer than it is today. People were more concerned with making a living than having a clean environment. But today, because we have greater wealth than we had then, we are better able to clean the environment.

Many Third World cities are polluted today. As they become wealthier, they, too, will take additional steps to protect their environment. As people become more affluent, they will insist on less pollution, and they will be willing to spend money, sometimes through their taxes, to help clean the air.

Michael Sanera and Jane S. Shaw, *Facts, Not Fear*, 1996.

Parents everywhere, it turns out, respond to a simple equation: Wealth permits them to raise fewer, more robust children. Producing food abundantly, in other words, is a highly effective way to limit population. But this sequel to the Malthusian story, in which humanity halts its own genetic sprawl, takes time to play out. For most of the last two centuries, mortality rates were dropping faster than fertility rates, so population grew. But in this century, mortality and fertility came into balance. Populations in the developed world have now stabilized. They will soon begin to shrink. If the trajectories of rising global affluence and falling fertility stay on their present course, world population—about 6 billion today—will peak at about 10 billion in 2050, and will then start shrinking.

The Real Meaning of Green

Green is what people become when they feel personally secure, when their own appetites have been satisfied, when they do not fear for the future, or for their own survival, or their children's. It is wealth that gives ordinary families the confidence to be generous to the world beyond. It is the rich who can be thin because they know they will always have plenty to eat. It is the rich who can cherish the wilderness because they no longer have to choose between their own survival and nature's.

"When the subdivisions advance, untold numbers of the plants and animals that shaped and filled our once-diverse landscapes go under."

Suburban Sprawl Threatens America's Wildlife

Kathrin Day Lassila

Kathrin Day Lassila is editor of the *Amicus Journal,* a publication of the Natural Resources Defense Council (NRDC). In the following viewpoint, she argues that poorly planned real estate development has resulted in urban and suburban sprawl that endangers wildlife by destroying habitat. Complex ecosystems are being lost to suburban houses, yards, and strip malls, she asserts. In addition, sprawl creates problems of air and water pollution. She calls for greater foresight in planning urban growth to protect endangered species.

As you read, consider the following questions:

1. What environmental problems does suburban sprawl create for native plants and animals, according to Lassila?
2. What are "weedy species" according to the author?
3. What steps does Lassila recommend to control sprawl?

Reprinted from Kathrin Day Lassila, "The New Suburbanites," *The Amicus Journal,* Summer 1999. Copyright © 1999 Kathrin Day Lassila. First published in *The Amicus Journal* (www.nrdc.org/amicus). Reprinted with permission from *The Amicus Journal.*

It was in the early 1980s, as Michael Klemens tells it now, that he started to realize that something was playing merry hell with his data.

Klemens, today an internationally known herpetologist with the Bronx, New York-based Wildlife Conservation Society, was collating and analyzing several years' worth of research on New England reptiles and amphibians. Since 1975, he had been wading streams and bushwhacking forests in search of turtles, salamanders, snakes, and frogs, in order to create a definitive study of their regional biogeography—where they lived and why. But when he tried to assemble the findings into a meaningful whole, he says, "I began to see a whole other dimension. It wasn't a two-dimensional problem: where are they and what's their history. There was a third dimension. There was all this noise coming in."

It took Klemens a few years before he felt certain of the source of the "noise" disrupting his data. Along the way were several eureka moments. One of these took place in the back rooms of the American Museum of Natural History, where samples of animals collected over decades are kept preserved for zoological research. Klemens had spent many days mapping the fauna of a stream network in southern New York State, in which the two-line salamander filled all available ecological niches for salamanders. The streams appeared healthy, the salamanders were thriving, and that should have been that. But then Klemens examined some dusty old jars that had been stored in the museum since the 1920s, when a predecessor of his had collected salamanders from the very same area. For stream after stream, the story was the same: there was one long-dead salamander floating in alcohol labeled "two-line," and another long-dead salamander labeled "dusky."

Where had all the dusky salamanders gone? Gradually, Klemens sorted out the answer. The two-line salamander lives happily in a variety of freshwater streams and rivers; the dusky needs springs and slow-flowing streams where organic debris can settle and collect. Everywhere the duskies used to live, suburban developments had moved in, clearing the uplands and putting down acres of asphalt. Instead of seeping into the ground, rainwater now sluiced directly off the asphalt and into the streams, where it speeded up water flows, caused floods, and scoured out stream beds. All of this was just fine with the two-line salamanders, especially when their salamander competition started to disappear—permanently, as it turned out.

This and other revelations spurred Klemens to devote the rest of his career to the impacts of environmentally damaging development on wildlife. As he notes, "We didn't call it 'sprawl' back then."

Poor Planning and Sprawl

Call it sprawl, call it poor land-use planning, call it the flight from inner cities and small towns into the spread-out developments that are mushrooming ever outward over forests and plains and farmland: Americans' footprint on our land has ballooned. It's not merely population growth, though our national surge from 150 million in 1950 to 250 million in 1990 is a major factor. It is also, inarguably, our lousy planning skills.

When it comes to looking at a chunk of territory and choosing judiciously where to build and where to renovate, where to encourage downtown reinvestment, and where to preserve farms and the natural landscape, Americans are ham-handed incompetents. We prefer just to throw up new buildings, new malls, and new roads haphazardly, and the bigger and farther apart, the better. The real estate industry itself says, in its 1997 annual report, "Many metropolitan areas have evolved as suburban expanses with no real center of gravity. Growth is diffused. New commercial centers sprout up randomly, surrounded by jerry-built communities . . . that often supplant the original central business district." And, in the 1999 annual report: "Suburbs struggle because they have let developers run amok."

In their recent book, *Once There Were Greenfields*, the Natural Resources Defense Council (NRDC) and the Surface Transportation Policy Project note that since 1980 the suburban populations of the major U.S. metropolitan areas have grown ten times faster than their central-city populations. The consequences the authors see for our land base are grave. From 1960 to 1990, the populations of metropolitan areas grew by less than half—but the amount of developed land in those areas doubled. Of all the land developed in the United States throughout its history, almost one-sixth was developed in the ten years from 1982 to 1992. In central Maryland, more land will be converted to housing between 1995 and 2020 than in the past three and a half centuries. It has been estimated that metropolitan Phoenix is developing open land at the rate of 1.2 acres per hour.

If Katharine Lee Bates were alive today, would it occur to her to write "America the Beautiful"? We are rapidly turning our purple mountain majesties and fruited plains into one endless blur of megahouses on sodded lawns, interrupted only by asphalt oceans of parking and asphalt rivers of new road that stretch, barren and full of traffic and shimmering with heat under the unshielded sun, from sea to shining sea.

Losing Wildlife

As Michael Klemens saw in data collected as early as 1975, one of the many things Americans are losing to our land appetite is our living natural heritage. When the subdivisions advance, untold numbers of the plants and animals that shaped and filled our once-diverse landscapes go under. "It's a problem that is extremely severe for wildlife," says Klemens. Other ecologists concur. "There's no doubt in my mind that sprawl is having a detrimental effect" on flora and fauna, says Ann Kinzig of Arizona State University. Joseph McAuliffe, an ecologist at the Desert Botanical Garden in Phoenix, calls sprawl "an environmental abomination."

For the most part, the losses are not of the kind to wring the public's heart. The grizzly bears, wolves, and buffalo, the great mammals that fire the imagination and easily gain admirers and sympathy, are largely not threatened by sprawl. They need so much space that they were driven out of the valleys and into remote preserves and mountaintops long ago. There are exceptions, among them medium-sized predators such as the Florida panther, whose southern Florida wetland and forest habitats are rapidly giving way to agricultural fields and residential developments. But for the most part, what is being lost to sprawl today is a different level of life, smaller, much less familiar to its human neighbors.

Their troubles come from a multiplicity of problems that accompany sprawl. More cars bring more air pollution. They create water pollution when the toxic residue of tires, gasoline, and oil washes off roadways and into streams. Streams and rivers must also cope with sewage effluent, with the larger burden of sediment that erodes off cleared land, with the loss of streamside plant communities, and with the harmful effects of large swaths of paving.

And then, of course, there are the two problems that Klemens considers particularly deadly. One is fragmentation of habitat. Roads and houses and malls break up ecosystems into parcels of land too small for their former occupants, or too far away from feeding or breeding grounds they depend on. Suzanne Fowle of the Massachusetts Natural Heritage and Endangered Species Program points out that for amphibians, even a road across their habitat may be enough to create genetically divergent groups. For long-lived, slowly reproducing species such as turtles, even an occasional road-kill death may be enough to start a population on a downward slide.

Replacing Diversity with Uniformity

The other problem is what Klemens calls the "generalization" of habitat. The ecosystems of this country are by nature extraordinarily diverse. But after the bulldozers leave, what's left is cleared space full of lawn grass, Norway maples, and pachysandra [a plant used for ground cover]. Even when the changes are less extreme, they are damaging. Klemens points to wetlands as a prime example of the generalization of habitat. "A lot of people are mouthing the phrase 'No net loss of wetlands,' but nobody is talking about the types of wetlands," he says. Environmental and development regulations do not protect minor wetlands, such as small vernal pools, which exist only in the springtime. And what protection there is, is inadequate. When highways, strip malls, and housing developments are built over structurally complex wetlands—fens, bogs, and other layered systems harboring a wide diversity of water-dependent life—developers must mitigate the damage. So they create ponds, which are simple systems. Says Klemens, "We are losing the complexity, the structure, the con-

Ruben Bolling. Copyright © 2000 Ruben Bolling. Reprinted with permission from Universal Press Syndicate.

nectedness of landscape wetlands at an alarming rate." This, as Joseph McAuliffe points out, is the real tragedy of sprawl: the loss of entire functioning landscapes.

In his twenty-five years of studying what happens to native species in New England when functioning landscapes are lost, Klemens has found a pattern. The numbers of wildlife do not necessarily decline; the overall biomass may stay the same or even increase. But the numbers of species plummet. As in the case of the two salamanders, a species that needs a specific and fragile kind of habitat, or that depends on more than one kind of habitat, will disappear. A competing species that can adapt to a broad array of habitats will take over.

Eventually, all that's left are what Klemens terms the "weedy species." "Call them 'subsidized species,'" he explains. "They get the competitive edge. They benefit from our activity. They are suited to living in the habitats we create." The extent of the takeover depends on the degree of habitat change. Some New York streams still have their two-line salamanders. Others have passed the point of no return. Says Klemens, "There is a threshold in landscape condition where everything starts to come unglued." In other words, in some highly modified suburban developments, there may be little wildlife left but pigeons, squirrels, and raccoons.

This pattern, Klemens believes, occurs all over the country. In Sonoma Valley, California, he found precisely the same trends where seasonal reed beds have been destroyed for "gentlemen's ranches" and replaced with year-round ponds. Rare native species such as the yellowleg frog, the Pacific pond turtle, and the endangered redleg frog are disappearing. The bullfrog, which is not even indigenous to the area, is moving in, preying on the native species, and spreading throughout the Sonoma Mountains.

Steward Pickett of the Institute of Ecosystem Studies says that many other studies have turned up evidence consistent with Klemens's findings, though he notes that few have studied the sprawl problem as systematically or as thoughtfully as Klemens. As one recent example, he mentions work by Helen Thompson, who found that gaps in forests near urban and suburban areas in the Baltimore region were being increasingly occupied by non-native vines.

"These problems are everywhere," comments Klemens. "It's the same basic pattern, because we're making the same kinds of choices with our ecosystems."

Possible Solutions

Is there an answer? There are many. There is no mystery about how to overhaul our lax land-use habits; the question has been thoroughly studied by many innovative planners and architects, and the solutions are well known. *Once There Were Greenfields* describes several "guiding principles" for reforming Americans' land-use habits, including the use of greenbelts and other land preserves, "infill" neighborhoods in central cities, and compact development patterns oriented to public transit rather than roads and highways. Compact development, the authors emphasize, does not mean cities full of high-rise apartment buildings; it can mean development that mixes, for instance, single-family houses and multi-family units such as townhouses.

How to put these answers into practice is more problematic. The environmental solution of last resort is the Endangered Species Act, which throws the force of federal law behind efforts to preserve the last remaining habitat of the last remaining individuals of a particular species. In the Pacific Northwest, nine species of salmon and steelhead trout were recently placed on the federal endangered species list. Since many of these species depend on rivers that already flow through metropolitan areas, the region may be forced to take steps to curb sprawl, among other problems, in order to protect the fish.

But the Endangered Species Act, vital as it is, cannot be the answer for the nation as a whole. We need to start protecting our unique species and unique places long before they reach the edge of disaster. More promising are the initiatives now springing up all over the country to bring genuine forethought and planning into land use. A dozen metropolitan areas have now instituted "urban growth boundaries," like that pioneered in Portland, Oregon, where regional government encourages growth within the boundary and discourages growth beyond it. Maryland has adopted a set of laws that, among other steps, withholds state funding for "growth-related" projects that do not meet specific criteria for housing density and other factors. In Georgia, which has undergone a revolution in public attitude toward sprawl, the legislature passed a law giving the governor extraordinary power to kill sprawl-producing projects and create sprawl-fighting ones in metropolitan Atlanta.

Reining in sprawl will take years or decades, especially as the problem and the planning infrastructure vary so much from community to community and region to region. "There isn't a single, magic answer," says NRDC attorney Kaid Benfield. "There's a need for creativity and many different approaches from communities, the private sector, the federal government, design companies. We know that the solution is smart growth. But we're all still working on the policy and economic climate that will make smart growth happen."

Hope in New England

From his own work, Michael Klemens offers the example of New York State's Great Swamp, a 4,000-acre wetland in the midst of five once-rural small towns, which are now suffering from inner decay and haphazard outward growth. For two years, Klemens's Metropolitan Conservation Alliance (MCA) has been working with the five towns to educate citizens about their wildlife heritage. Volunteers have taken part in wildlife tracking programs, workshops, school projects, and other activities. Now that community interest is high and a sound database of wildlife information exists, the project is moving to a new phase. MCA is beginning to train community officials to use detailed wildlife and habitat data in land-use planning that preserves biodiversity. Moreover, the five towns are considering setting up an intermunicipal council for wildlife conservation, transportation, and infrastructure.

Overwhelming as the sprawl problem seems, Klemens is full of optimism. Especially in New England, where the political system gives local decisionmakers great power in land-use decisions, he sees "a huge uncharted area" for progress through training community officials in the ecology of their area and bringing them together for regional planning. "I enjoy my work, because we've had success," says Klemens—who has seen success not only in the MCA projects, but also in his own town, where he serves as chair of the planning commission. "We have to recognize that we can't change the ecological mandate of the land. We have to work within it. And it *can* be done."

"When it comes to deer, suburban habitat is more productive than the forests of New York."

Suburban Sprawl Does Not Threaten America's Wildlife

Jane S. Shaw

Suburban sprawl does not spell the end to wildlife because humans and nature are learning to coexist in many metropolitan areas, argues Jane S. Shaw in the following viewpoint. In many places where suburban areas have taken over agricultural land, forested areas have expanded and populations of deer and other animals have risen. Individuals and businesses have taken steps to make yards and other private property parcels more hospitable to wildlife. Shaw is a senior associate of the Political Economy Research Center, a research and education foundation that supports free market solutions to environmental problems.

As you read, consider the following questions:
1. What is the "normal" state of nature, according to Shaw?
2. What does Shaw consider to the be the most objective way to examine the impact of suburban growth on nature?
3. What species of animals have been especially successful at living in suburban areas, according to the author?

Excerpted from Jane S. Shaw, "Nature in the Suburbs," in *A Guide to Smart Growth*, edited by Jane S. Shaw and Ronald D. Utt. Copyright © 2000 The Heritage Foundation and The Political Economy Research Center. Reprinted with permission from The Heritage Foundation.

Environmentalists criticize urban sprawl on many grounds. One of the most emotionally charged criticisms is that sprawl eats up land that otherwise would provide habitat for wildlife or, at the very least, serve as productive farmland.

"Sprawl, by definition, fragments landscapes—and fragmented landscapes are the biggest threat to America's wildlife heritage," writes Carl Pope, executive director of the Sierra Club. As he explains, such landscapes are "very good for the most adaptable and common creatures—raccoons, deer, sparrows, starlings, and sea gulls," but "devastating for wildlife that is more dependent upon privacy, seclusion, and protection from such predators as dogs and cats."

Other commentators are even more disparaging of the wild animals that survive in the suburbs. They call them "weedy species." The term usually refers to exotic, non-native species like the kudzu vine that invade new areas and then are hard to get rid of, but the name also has been applied to a larger number of species that are not necessarily invaders. Nature writer David Quammen defines weedy species as animals and plants that "reproduce quickly, disperse widely when given a chance, tolerate a fairly broad range of habitat conditions, take hold in strange places, succeed especially in disturbed ecosystems, and resist eradication once they're established." They are found in "human-dominated terrain because in crucial ways they resemble *Homo sapiens:* aggressive, versatile, prolific, and ready to travel."

Weedy Species?

Although it is true that animals like grizzly bears and elk are not likely to be found in the suburbs, humans may be more compatible with wildlife than most people think. This viewpoint will explore the evidence. To begin with, the impression that nothing is left but weedy species deserves careful scrutiny. Yes, such animals may be "common" and "adaptable" (they are "common" almost by definition), but this does not mean that nobody wants them—quite the contrary, in fact. Nor is it evident that growing suburbs necessarily push out large animals. In some cases, there were few before the suburbs arose because the land was being cultivated intensively. In other cases, large animals still lurk nearby.

In fact, one observer of sprawl sees the new suburbs as abounding in wildlife—at least in comparison to the urban areas in which most Americans grew up. In his book *Edge City*, journalist Joel Garreau discusses the newest suburbs, the towns on the edge of metropolitan areas to which people increasingly gravitate. Garreau says that this distant suburban growth has put people back in touch with nature.

In these new cities, "more humans are getting closer to other high-order species than at any time in the past century," he contends. Garreau claims that for the first time since the industrial revolution, "the majority of the American people—whether they know it or not or like it or not—may soon be sharing their territory with fairly large wild animals."

Change is occurring in America's growing metropolitan areas and, as every ecologist knows, all change helps some species and hurts others. "The 'normal' state of nature is not one of balance and repose," says science writer Stephen Budiansky; "the 'normal' state is to be recovering from the last disaster. In most ecosystems the interval between disturbances—fire, frost, flood, windstorm—is almost always less than the life span of an individual member of the dominant species. So much for balance."

When people move onto what once was rural land, they provide a new form of disturbance. They modify the landscape by building more streets, more parking lots, and more buildings. Wetlands may be drained, hayfields may disappear, trees may be cut down, and pets may proliferate. At the same time, however, the new residents will build ponds, establish gardens, plant trees, and set up bird nesting-boxes. Ornamental nurseries and truck farms may replace cropland, and parks may replace hedgerows. The new ecology is different, but not necessarily worse. . . .

Historically Changing Environments

Perhaps the most objective way to look at the impact of suburban growth on nature is to recognize that each area has a unique past and its own changes. Although some changes may impoverish wildlife, others may lead to a more ecologically diverse setting.

One example of the positive impact of growth is the rebound of the endangered Key deer, a small white-tailed deer found only in Florida and named for the Florida Keys. According to *Audubon* magazine, the Key deer is experiencing a "remarkable recovery." The news report continues: "Paradoxically, part of the reason for the deer's comeback may lie in the increasing development of the area." Paraphrasing the remarks of Roel Lopez, the researcher at Texas A&M University who quantified the deer population, the reporter says that human development "tends to open up overgrown forested areas and provide vegetation at deer level—the same factors fueling deer population booms in suburbs all over the country."

James R. Dunn, a geologist who has pieced together some of the wildlife history around Albany, New York, has a similar analysis to explain what he views as a proliferation of wildlife in suburban areas. He describes several important land-use changes that occurred during the past few hundred years in that region. The first occurred when colonial settlers farmed the area, probably after extensively logging the forest. Later, during the 19th century, as farming shifted westward to the more fertile fields of the Midwest, many New York farms were abandoned. The forest began to grow back.

During the second half of the 20th century, the gradual growth of population led suburbs to develop around Albany. As they moved out, people began to settle this land again. Some of it had reforested; some was still meadow, and some was still agricultural. "During my years as a geologist in this area," writes Dunn, "I discovered that many roads on old topographic maps are no longer used. These roads serviced a checkerboard of farms, orchards, and grazing lands during the 1800s and until about 1920. The roads were abandoned when agricultural lands were no longer needed."

Dunn sees this process as creating today's "suburban" mixture of forest, field, home, and street. In his view, the result is an enriched habitat, not a diminished one. His backyard, he claims, has more than 50 bird species.

Dunn goes further. He contends that when it comes to deer, suburban habitat is more productive than the forests of New York, such as those of the Adirondack Mountains. Dunn cites statistics on the harvest of buck deer reported by the New York State government to argue his point. He observes that since 1970 the deer population multiplied 7.1 times in suburban areas (an increase of 610 percent) and only 3.4 times (an increase of 240 percent) in the state overall. (See Chart.)

Increase in Buck Deer Harvest in New York State Is Greatest in Urbanized Counties

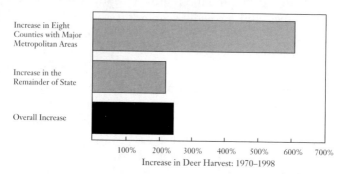

New York State Department of Conservation, *New York State Deer Take by County and Town*, 1998.

He explains that the forests have been allowed to regrow without logging or burning, so that today they lack the "edge" that allows sunlight in and fosters vegetation suitable for deer. That is why the counties with big cities (and therefore with suburbs) have seen a greater increase in deer populations than have the isolated, forested rural counties.

Certainly, the regrowth of Eastern forests is a dramatic occurrence that unfolded throughout most of the 20th century. In 1991, a research organization in Washington, D.C., Resources for the Future, estimated that the percent of land forested in New Hampshire had increased from 50 percent in the 1880s to 86 percent 100 years later. Forested land in Connecticut, Massachusetts, and Rhode Island increased from 35 percent to 59 percent over that same period."

Environmentalist Bill McKibben exulted in this "unintentional and mostly unnoticed renewal of the rural and mountainous East" in a 1995 *Atlantic Monthly* article. Calling the change "the great environmental story of the United States, and in some ways of the whole world," he added, "Here, where 'suburb' and 'megalopolis' were added to the world's vocabulary, an explosion of green is under way." Along with the reforestation come the animals: McKibben cites a moose "ten miles from Boston," as well as an eastern United States full of black bears, deer, alligators, and perhaps even mountain lions. Unlike Dunn, McKibben does not differentiate among the kinds of land—full forest or fragmented forest—but he paints a dramatic picture of new, emergent wilderness.

Abundance of Deer

These days, deer are the most prominent species proliferating in the suburbs. The increase in the number of deer in the United States is so great that many people, especially wildlife professionals, are trying to figure out what to do about them. In 1997, the Wildlife Society, a professional association of wildlife biologists, devoted a special 600-page issue of its *Bulletin* to the subject of "Deer Overabundance." The lead article noted, "We hear more each year about the high costs of crop and tree-seedling damage, deer-vehicle collisions, and nuisance deer in suburban locales." Insurance companies are worried about the increase in damage that results when automobiles and deer (and similar-sized animals) collide. And there are fears that the increase in deer in populated areas means that the deer tick could be causing the rise in reported cases of Lyme disease.

Yes, the proliferation of deer poses problems, as does the restoration of geese, whose flocks can foul ponds and lawns, and of beaver, which can cut down groves of trees. Yet these problems are manageable, and their very existence undercuts claims that suburban growth destroys wildlife. The proliferation of deer is a wildlife success story ("one of the premier examples of successful wildlife management," says Robert J. Warren, editor of the *Wildlife Society Bulletin*). Noting that today's deer population in the United States may be as high as 25 million, Richard Nelson, writing in *Sports Afield*, says:

> Just a few decades ago, if anyone had predicted that deer would join robins and gray squirrels as denizens of the suburbs . . . that sage would likely have been shrugged off as a lunatic. But in many parts of the country, deer have become

so abundant that they're causing serious problems on the roadways and in our neighborhoods, natural preserves and farmlands.

Not surprisingly, people have mixed feelings about the deer. In the *Wildlife Society Bulletin,* Dale R. McCullough and his colleagues reported on a survey of households in El Cerrito and Kensington, two communities near Berkeley, California. Of those who responded to the survey, 50 percent reported seeing deer "frequently" and 25 percent "occasionally." Twenty-eight percent reported severe damage to vegetation by the deer, and 25 percent reported moderate damage. Forty-two percent liked having the deer around, while 35 percent disliked them and 24 percent were indifferent. The authors summarized the findings by saying: "As expected, some residents loved deer, whereas others considered them 'hoofed rats.'"

This mixture of attitudes is not merely a California phenomenon. Two members of the Missouri Department of Conservation report "a management dilemma" in urban areas where deer are proliferating and hunting is not allowed. Yet, in spite of problems such as auto accidents and destruction of gardens and native vegetation, "surveys of Missouri urbanites indicate white-tailed deer are highly popular." In fact, they report that the deer was voted "the wild animal that urban Missourians most enjoyed viewing."

Other Proliferating Species

Of course, deer are not the only wild animals willing to live around growing urban areas. Joel Garreau cites black bears, red-tailed hawks, peregrine falcons, and beaver in his list of animals that find niches in the new, distant suburbs. Garreau still considers these suburbs a "far less diverse ecology than what was there before." However, "if you measure it by the standard of city, it is a far more diverse ecology than anything humans have built in centuries, if not millennia," he writes.

James Dunn lists the species that inhabit the suburbs in his region in addition to deer: birds such as robins, woodpeckers, chickadees, grouse, finches, hawks, crows, and nuthatches, as well as squirrels, chipmunks, opossums, raccoons, foxes, and rabbits. Deer attract coyotes, too. According to a 1999 article in *Audubon*, biologists estimate that the coyote population (observed in all states except Hawaii) is about double what it was in 1850.

Although deer and coyotes can be described as common, adaptable, and perhaps even "weedy species," a more accurate term is the one coined by University of Florida biologist Larry Harris, "meso-mammals," or mammals of medium size. They do not need broad territory for roaming to find food, as moose and grizzly bears do. They can find places to feed, nest, and thrive in the suburbs, especially those where gardens flourish.

Not all the wild animals who turn up near home sites and commercial areas are small. In fast-growing Orange County, California, deer serve as prey for mountain lions, according to studies by Paul Beier, a professor at the University of California at Berkeley. In 1994, two people in the area were killed by mountain lions. Although mountain lions had been recognized as present in the nearby Mount Hamilton region, by 1997 "the number of reports has increased considerably, and it seems likely that resident animals are present."

An article in a Montana newspaper, also citing Paul Beier's work, reported that mountain lion encounters are increasing around the country. The article noted that according to "conventional wisdom," the encounters occur because more people are moving into the lions' habitat; however, the author says that the reverse is true also. Lions "are spending more time in what has long been considered human habitat, our cities and towns and subdivisions." Even in the East, mountain lions may be coming back. Bill McKibben reported in 1995 that the Eastern Puma Research Network had been told of 1,800 puma (a mountain lion) sightings during the previous 10 years. The National Wildlife Federation reports a resurgence of cougars (another mountain lion) in California, where they are endangering bighorn sheep in the Sierra Nevadas.

Although black bears are smaller than the relatively rare and dangerous grizzlies, they can be sizable, and they appear to be moving into urban areas, too. Writing in *The New York Times*, reporter Robert Hanley noted that a 175-pound black bear was discovered in "the heart of the business district" of

West Haven, Connecticut. "The world of wildlife is far different from what it was a generation ago," Hanley noted, "as more housing eats into once distant wilderness. All sorts of species no longer stay secluded in deep woods." He specifically cited "moose on the developing outer fringes of suburbia; coyotes, fox, deer and the ubiquitous Canada geese in older suburban towns; bears and turkeys in cities."

Even elk have been infiltrating subdivisions in Jefferson County, Colorado. According to the *Rocky Mountain News*, state wildlife officials estimate that 2,500 elk live in the area between Denver and the Continental Divide. "The increase has occurred entirely in residential subdivisions such as Evergreen Meadows, not in the area's vast expanses of national forests, according to state wildlife biologist Janet George," the article stated.

The renewal of wildlife is not limited to the United States. A news report in the *Sunday Times* of London reported that seals are again swimming up the Thames River and entering London.

Wild Backyards

Some environmental groups acknowledge the richness, or potential richness, of the suburban environment. A project of the National Wildlife Federation is called "Backyard Wildlife Habitat." It is both an informational program and one that certifies backyards as attractive for wildlife.

For example, one Colorado backyard habitat certified by the National Wildlife Federation started with a pond, berry bushes, and spruces. Today the owner finds mallard and wood ducks, herons, hawks, kingfishers and other large birds, snakes, foxes, and skunks on her property. She has chickadees in a nest box and finches in a thistle feeder. "Before" and "after" photos on the National Wildlife Web site are impressive.

Through its Web site, the National Wildlife Federation offers advice to amateur naturalists on how to develop certifiable wildlife-friendly yards. Would-be habitat builders are led through the "basics" of improving their backyards. Other advice is more complex. In "Learn How to Build a Simple Pond," Doug Inkley, a senior scientist for the Federation, describes how to design a pond to include fish and frogs. . . .

Meanwhile, studies are beginning to show that even urban areas are richer in wildlife than most people assume. *Science* magazine reported on a six-year, $4.4 million study of animal species in Phoenix, Arizona. Researchers identified "over 75 species of bees, 200 species of birds, and hundreds of insect species within metropolitan Phoenix," reported freelance writer Keith Kloor. "True, some heavyweights are absent," the author notes. Bighorn sheep and "other animals that need room to roam aren't going to make it in Phoenix," he says. However, he quotes Charles Redman, an anthropologist at Arizona State University who helped oversee the study: "The simple notion that a city diminishes biodiversity is wrong."

Apparent Compatibility

What Americans are seeing is an apparent compatibility— albeit perhaps an uneasy one—of animals and humans in growing metropolitan areas. This should not really surprise us. Suburbs have grown in large measure because people have the wealth and the mobility to move into less-dense environments. Economic studies show that as income rises, people begin to take better care of their surroundings and show greater interest in protecting their environment. Although they may rely on shopping malls and drive on highways, they also like open space, gardens, and trees—all characteristics that are likely to attract or nurture wild animals.

Studies show the connection between increasing wealth and environmental protection in a variety of settings, from controlling air pollution to passing laws that protect open space. The connection is even illustrated by the fact that environmentalists tend to have significantly higher incomes than other Americans. A typical reader of *Sierra*, the magazine of the Sierra Club, earns nearly twice the average income of Americans. It is intuitively clear that for many people one reason to move to the suburbs, including the distant suburbs, is to be closer to nature.

Some entrepreneurs, responding to this interest in nature, are making deliberate efforts to maintain the natural environment when they develop home sites. In the West, entrepreneurs are integrating homes with habitat for wildlife, including such large animals as elk and bears. . . .

One of the most intriguing ways to combine nature and residences is by restoring native plants. Ron Bowen, president of Prairie Restorations, Inc., is a pioneer in this endeavor. On his "farm" in southern Minnesota, Bowen raises plants like wild rye and thimbleweed, vegetation native to the prairies and savannahs of the Midwest. Until recently, residents routinely replaced such plants on their lawns with imported vegetation, such as Kentucky blue grass. But some years ago, Bowen dreamed of bringing back native vegetation by designing landscapes that resembled the traditional fields of southern Minnesota. Today, his restorations can be found on the lawns of corporate headquarters and private homeowners. (Bowen sells a "plant-it-yourself" package of seeds for the less affluent client).

Similar efforts are being made by entrepreneurs and nonprofit organizations around the country. Yet the phenomenon of privately restored mini-prairies cannot occur without the open space that suburbs make possible. Maintaining "native prairie" means setting fires periodically—as American Indians did—to rejuvenate the vegetation. Bowen's efforts would be severely restricted in a dense urban setting. And while it is possible for governments and non-profit organizations to create prairie preserves in large areas, only low-density suburbs can bring the experience of prairie life to individuals on a day-to-day basis.

In addition to such entrepreneurial efforts, citizens in jurisdictions throughout the country are taking political action in an attempt to set aside more open space—another sign that increasingly affluent Americans are willing to spend money to maintain natural habitat where they live. In 1998, voters in many states passed ballot measures to provide funds for additional open space set-asides. In his 1991 book, Joel Garreau remarked that the New Jersey state plan (a growth-management strategy) urged company headquarters to become "refuges for wildlife" and new residential developments to be "clustered and adjoin protected natural streams and wooded areas." The opportunity for intimacy with nature is one that many people welcome, and one to which developers and corporate executives are responding.

Living Harmoniously with Wildlife

Whatever happens to resolve the issue of sprawl, a major concern in the coming years certainly will be how to live harmoniously with a reviving natural world of wildlife. Indeed, unless most people are willing to give up their broad lawns and single-family homes, the issue of integrating wildlife with day-to-day human life may well turn out to be more compelling, and perhaps more divisive, than today's controversy over sprawl.

Periodical Bibliography

The following articles have been selected to supplement the diverse views presented in this chapter. Addresses are provided for periodicals not indexed in the *Readers' Guide to Periodical Literature*, the *Alternative Press Index*, the *Social Sciences Index*, or the *Index to Legal Periodicals and Books*.

America	"Welcome, Adnan Mevic!" November 20, 1999.
Amicus Journal	"Car Talk: Environmentalists Wrestle with the Car Problem," Fall 1999.
Robin Andersen	"Road to Ruin," *Extra!* September/October 1998.
Linda Baker	"Malling America," *E Magazine*, May/June 2000.
F. Kaid Benfield	"Once There Were Greenfields," *Forum for Applied Research and Public Policy*, Fall 1999.
Ralph Kinney Bennet	"Electric Cars? Fahgedaboudit!" *Reader's Digest*, January 1998.
Jacques Cousteau, interviewed by Nathan Gardels	"Consumer Society Is the Enemy," *New Perspectives Quarterly*, vol. 16, no. 2, 1999.
Thomas J. DiLorenzo	"The Myth of Suburban Sprawl," *USA Today*, May 2000.
Mark Hertsgaard	"Will We Run Out of Gas?" *Time*, November 8, 1999.
Peter Huber	"Wealth Is Not the Enemy of the Environment," *Vital Speeches*, April 1, 2000.
Fred Lucas	"Eco-Friendly Sport Utility," *Insight on the News*, August 16, 1999. Available from 21 Congress St., Salem, MA 01970.
Jason Mark	"Who's In the Driver's Seat?" *Dollars and Sense*, July/August 1998.
Michael Massing	"Stalled in Paradise," *American Prospect*, Spring 2000.
Norman Meyers	"Sustainable Consumption," *Science*, March 31, 2000.
Randal O'Toole	"The Coming War on the Automobile," *Liberty*, March 1998. Available from Liberty Foundation, 1018 Water St., Suite 201, Port Townsend, WA 98368.
Mark Sagoff	"Do We Consume Too Much?" *Atlantic Monthly*, June 1997.

CHAPTER 4

What Principles and Values Should Guide American Environmental Policy?

Chapter Preface

In an influential 1968 essay, ecologist Garret Hardin popularized the expression "tragedy of the commons." His example was a village pasture that anyone could use. Sheepherders, Hardin argued, would rationally decide to graze as many animals that they owned as they could on the commons, since they would reap the benefits from each additional animal while the costs of their grazing were shared by all. But if all herders did the same, the pasture would be overgrazed and destroyed.

The village pasture in Hardin's example can be interpreted to represent the environment in general—a sort of global commons that is used jointly by all and in which the activities of one can affect many. For instance, the air we breathe is a "commons" that nobody owns but everybody uses. A factory owner can rationally decide to pollute that air because the costs of pollution would be shared with everyone in the vicinity, while the factory owner reaps all the benefits. But if everyone draws the same individual conclusion, the result can be disastrous for all. As in the example of the village pasture, the rational decision of individuals regarding resources held in common can lead to the depletion of those resources and to ecological ruin.

People have drawn differing conclusions regarding environmental policy from this example. Hardin himself considered it a warning against human overpopulation, which he believed threatened to overrun the global "commons." Some argue that resources held in common require collective—not individual—decisions, and call for government regulations and international treaties limiting pollution and resource exploitation. Others contend that the problem lies in the collective ownership of resources. If the village commons were divided among private owners, they say, owners would take care of their own parcels because the costs of overgrazing would be borne by them alone. Likewise, environmental solutions are not to be found in more government regulations, but in promoting private ownership of land and other resources, thereby forcing polluters to pay the costs of their own pollution. The viewpoints in this chapter feature differing perspectives on the "tragedy of the commons" and on other important questions regarding United States environmental policy.

1

"Economists are increasingly discovering examples of how the creation of . . . private . . . property rights can solve environmental problems."

Free-Market Principles Should Guide Environmental Policy

Terry L. Anderson and Jane S. Shaw

Environment and conservation policies in the United States over the past few decades have been equated in the public's mind with government action to regulate pollution and manage publicly owned land. In the following viewpoint, Terry L. Anderson and Jane S. Shaw argue that a growing number of economists have called for alternative approaches to environmental protection and that basic theories on how free markets operate can explain and provide solutions to environmental problems. Extending private property rights to parks and wilderness areas, in this view, can be superior to government management and regulation in conserving natural habitats and protecting the environment. Anderson is executive director and Shaw a senior associate of the Political Economy Research Center, an organization that promotes free-market approaches to conservation.

As you read, consider the following questions:
1. What fundamental principles concerning scarcity do most economists share, according to Anderson and Shaw?
2. What examples do Anderson and Shaw provide of how private property rights have enhanced environmental protection?

M any mainstream economists have found that the well-accepted principles that explain market behavior and underlie prosperity also explain environmental problems and offer ways to solve them.

Free market environmentalism is based on the economic way of thinking, which all economists share. Milton Friedman, a leading free-market economist, once observed that he and Paul Samuelson, a leading economist of the Keynesian school, which has more confidence in government, differ in their opinions on many topics, but they tend to speak with one voice when they talk about human behavior with non-economist social scientists. Both Friedman and Samuelson share the economic way of thinking, which relies on a few useful principles. These can be summarized as follows:

1. Because of scarcity, we cannot have all that we want, so we must make choices.

2. Choices require that we give up one good to get another; in other words, all things have opportunity costs.

3. In making choices, people weigh the costs and benefits of their decisions—to themselves, but not necessarily to others.

4. Hence, incentives—the costs and benefits as people perceive them for themselves—affect individual and group decisions.

Points of Disagreement

While these principles are at the heart of economics, applying them does spark disagreements over how well market transactions (that is, trades made voluntarily) incorporate the costs and benefits of individual decisions. Do individuals really bear the costs of their decisions and reap the benefits? Or are some costs and benefits borne and received by "outside" parties? And, if market decisions do leave out some costs and benefits, what should be done about it? These questions frequently arise in connection with environmental matters.

For example, when a person purchases a pound of bacon, the market price reflects the costs of marketing, transporting, or butchering the pig. But it may not reflect the costs to the neighbors of odor wafting from a large swine feeding operation. When a person donates money to purchase wildlife habitat, the individual receives satisfaction, a benefit, from the donation. But others get benefits, too, from the increase in wildlife or the preservation of open space. Thus, those who do *not* donate get a "free ride" from those who do. To summarize economists' views, the concern is that when costs are not taken into account, too much of a good thing such as bacon will be produced because others bear some of the costs. And when benefits are not taken into account, too little of a good thing such as wildlife habitat will be provided because the benefits are received by "free riders" who do not have to pay for them.

In the past, many mainstream economists took the position that private decisions fail to consider many of the environmental costs and benefits of a transaction. They called such situations "market failures" and thought governmental decisions could correct them by taking more costs and benefits into account. They assumed that government officials are not motivated by self-interest in the same way that individual market actors are.

Over the years, however, many economists discovered that in addition to market failures there are government failures. The Keynesianism of Paul Samuelson, which was skeptical of markets and confident in governments, has given ground to Milton Friedman's free-market economics, which is skeptical of government and confident about markets. Both views are mainstream today. In fact, Keynesianism, according to many, is on the wane. . . .

When it comes to environmental economics, the change has been especially dramatic. Keynesian economist Lester Thurow may well have reflected the views of the mainstream of the profession in 1980 when he wrote that a clean environment consists of economic goods and services that "cannot be achieved without collective action." But free market environmentalists have shown the rest of the profession that this is not necessarily true. The prime cause of environmental problems is not "market failure," as many economists thought, but the absence of markets—more specifically, the absence of private ownership, the foundation of markets. While economists have long known that transactions based on private property are imperfect, many now recognize that the absence of private property and therefore of markets distorts incentives even more than do problems of incorporating costs and benefits in market transactions.

Tragedy of the Commons

The idea that something that no one owns is badly treated goes back at least as far as [the ancient Greek philosopher] Aristotle, who wrote that "what is common to many is taken least care of, for all men have greater regard for what is their own than for what they possess in common with others." We are indebted to a biologist, Garrett Hardin, for articulating it anew. The "tragedy of the commons," described in a seminal 1968 article in *Science*, underlies most environmental problems.

Hardin describes a commonly-owned pasture. In such a pasture, the individual who adds a cow (when the pasture is full) receives the full benefit of the additional cow, but does not pay the full cost of using up the pasture. That cost is shared among all the villagers who own livestock. The result, as long as access is open to all, will be overgrazing and ultimately destruction of the commons.

In other words, the individual who adds another cow receives full benefits but does not pay the full cost of his or her action of adding the cow. In a commons with open access, each person has an incentive to take action that is costly for the group as a whole because the cost is shared while the benefits are individually enjoyed. The tragedy occurs because perverse incentives lead to destruction.

For economists, the "tragedy of the commons" illustrates what happens when an individual does not pay the full social costs of a decision. Everyone who has spent much time in public parks knows that people treat them negligently, allowing litter to accumulate and crowding to occur. Park visitors have little incentive to pay the cost of keeping parks clean. A person who tosses only one or two scraps in a large park is contributing only a small part of the total cost of a messy park. The benefit (in a word, laziness) goes to the individual, while the cost (a littered park) is spread among many. Furthermore, there is no owner who benefits financially by making sure that the experience pleases visitors (and thus is not too crowded).

Air and water are polluted because they, too, are a commons. They have no owners to keep people from using them for waste, so polluters gain the benefits of getting rid of their waste while sharing the cost with many others.

Another example of the commons is wildlife. The bison came close to extinction and the passenger pigeon died out because they were commonly owned. Hunters obtained the benefits of killing what they could, while the cost—the gradual decline in numbers to near-extinction—was shared among everyone. Hunters wanted them, and because they were commonly owned no one had an incentive to protect a herd or a flock for the future. Today, much wildlife is endangered because it is a commons.

The Role of Government

The debate over free market environmentalism centers on how to eliminate the tragedy of the commons or, more broadly, how to get the incentives right. Should a government, with coercive powers and collective decision-making, regulate the commons? Or should efforts be made to allow private property to regulate the commons? In the past, most mainstream economists assumed that the government could regulate the commons, including the air and water that had become polluted. But today economists realize that government regulation poses severe problems of its own.

Joseph Stiglitz, a prominent Keynesian economist who served as chairman of President Bill Clinton's Council of Economic Advisers, wrote after his stint in government that he had achieved a "better understanding of government failures to counterbalance the market failures that have occupied so much of my thinking as a professional economist." He went on to say that "misaligned incentives" were at the heart of the difficulties he faced as he tried to improve government policies. Such incentives "can induce government officials to take actions that are not, in any sense, in the public interest.". . .

Economists began abandoning their market failure arguments and began exploring "government failure." They noticed that regulatory agencies could be "captured" by special interests, so that the agency was no longer pursuing the public interest but, rather, protecting the firms it was supposed to be regulating.

A growing number of economists, led by George Stigler, began to develop theories for why this occurred. . . .

Comparing the Visions of Environmentalists and Conservationists

	Environmentalists	Conservationists
World View	It is a world of problems.	It is a world of opportunity.
Relationship Between Humans and the Environment	Nature is best left undisturbed, because humans harm the environment; people commit a "crime" when they disturb nature.	The balance of nature *includes* humans; solutions to environmental problems can be balanced with human needs and development objectives.
Perception of Risk	Every risk is avoidable; the federal government should invest in eliminating risks at any cost.	A totally risk-free society is not possible, but regulators squander valuable resources pursuing one.
View of Regulation	Regulations are necessary and good.	Regulations have good and bad effects; sometimes they create more risk and offer less protection.
Solutions to Environmental Problems	Centralized command-and-control regulation is necessary; federal bureaucrats and administrative agencies must have authority to allocate resources as they see fit.	A wealthier society is a healthier society; those who have ownership in a resource need freedom and incentives to create and implement efficient, effective solutions.
Stewardship of Resources	Collective stewardship of environmental resources is far superior to private ownership.	Private ownership promotes individual responsibility and sensible stewardship.
Property Rights	Private property is subject to government's objectives, no matter who owns it.	No one shall be denied the reasonable use of his or her property without just compensation
The Role of Consumers in the Free Market	Bureaucrats know what's best for consumers and their families. People cannot be trusted to make wise environmental decisions.	If given the choice, consumers will make wise environmental decisions within the marketplace.

Heritage Foundation, *Issues 2000: The Candidate's Briefing Book*, 2000.

Environmental economics is evolving in the same direction, toward recognition of problems with government regulation and toward greater respect for the marketplace. Building on the work of Mancur Olson and George Stigler, economists such as Sam Peltzman and Gary Becker have pointed out that not just industries but other small, concentrated interest groups such as environmental activists can control regulatory policies. When this happens, the results are not necessarily in the public interest. . . .

Free-Market Solutions

Free-market environmentalists have long been aware of the problems of government decision making. They propose dealing with the potential tragedy of the commons by establishing private property rights. Private ownership makes people accountable. People must bear the costs of actions that decrease the value of the resources they use and they can reap the rewards of actions that increase the value of the resources. If they neglect what they have, the property will fall in value. If owners husband what they have, it will grow in value. These facts provide incentives for good stewardship.

Economists are increasingly discovering examples of how the creation of (or recognition of) private or quasi-private property rights can solve environmental problems. For example, in parts of Africa, elephant herds are declining in population, largely because they are commonly owned and their ivory is sought after. Yet in southern Africa, where elephant herds are, in effect, owned by the surrounding villagers, elephant numbers are increasing rather than falling. The now-famous CAMPFIRE program in Zimbabwe provides villagers with meat, hides, and cash from legal elephant hunts. These benefits provide an incentive for the villagers to protect elephants for the future so that they will reap rewards in the future as well as the present. People who previously allowed poaching now take great care of the elephants in their region.

To the extent that the elephants are private property—and of course the elephants remain wild, but the villagers have quasi-ownership—the villagers in Zimbabwe bear the costs and benefits of their decisions. If they cooperate with poachers and let the elephants be killed in excessive numbers, they will feel the costs. They will lose the benefits of having elephants in the future. Because they are, in essence, owners of the elephants, they make sure that there will be enough elephants so that there can be legal hunts from which they earn goods and money.

Many other examples of "privatizing," or partly privatizing, the commons can be found. New York City recently gave day-to-day responsibility for the city's crown jewel, Central Park, to a private nonprofit group, the Central Park Conservancy. The city found that it could not adequately maintain the quality of this park (actual ownership remains with the city government, however).

This followed by a few years a move by private businesses surrounding Bryant Park in midtown Manhattan to join together to restore the park. Because Bryant Park was a "commons" with open access, it had attracted drug dealers and drug addicts. Few others ventured near the park, which became seedy and neglected. The businesses formed a district (this district is public, but small and similar to a private organization). They cleaned up the park, hired security guards to patrol it, and began to restore it to a park that thousands enjoy. In both cases, the parks were not literally privately owned, but they were managed with owner-like concern.

A historical example, Ravenna Park in Seattle, illustrates the process in reverse. In the early twentieth century, private owners saved beautiful Douglas fir trees from the loggers' saw. After the city took over the park, however, the magnificent forest was cut down, and it is now just another city park with playgrounds and tennis courts. During the 1970s, it attracted homeless people and criminals.

Even water is sometimes privately owned, or nearly so. In England, while most water is publicly owned, fishing rights on most rivers and streams (but not in coastal fisheries) are private. This right gives anglers an opportunity to protect streams from pollution. The anglers have an incentive to seek out polluters and sue, if necessary, to protect their valuable fishing assets.

In the western United States, people who divert water for irrigation and other purposes have legal rights to use the diverted water. By trading those rights, they allow water to be used more efficiently, with less need for new dams and irrigation canals. Furthermore, while government efforts to save declining salmon stocks have been expensive and largely fruitless, a number of people have worked out water trades that save salmon. . . .

None of this is to say that private ownership is always possible for all commons. Applying private ownership to air basins, for example, is not conceivable today, and thus we rely on government regulation to clean up the air above Los Angeles. Government regulation may be a necessary second-best solution. But even here it is possible to define specific airsheds or basins and manage them in ways that private owners would. For example, an airshed manager could draw revenues from emitters on the basis of the amount of the air basin they used. The manager could search for low-cost opportunities for keeping the air clean and reward those who took advantage of them.

We should not ignore the possibility for evolution to private property rights. When settlers first began managing cattle on the Great Plains in the mid-1800s, establishing property rights to land would have seemed impossible. The spaces were vast, and there were few trees to build fences with. But as the potential value of enclosed land increased, an economic incentive developed that led to a low-cost way of eliminating the tragedy of the commons—barbed wire. Once effective fences could be set up, people's property could be marked and protected. In a parallel way, new technology may make it possible to trace sources of pollution so that the "owners" of that pollution can be identified. If they can be identified, the "owners" can be held accountable for harm they may cause. Chemical tracers introduced into smokestacks have been used on an experimental basis to track pollutants.

The Global Picture

There is now international evidence that the protection of private property rights is closely linked to environmental quality. Seth Norton, a professor of economics at Wheaton College, found measures of the extent to which countries have property rights protection and then looked at how this protection correlated with measures of environmental quality.

In nations where property rights are well protected, roughly 93 percent of the population has access to safe drinking water, compared with only about 60 percent of the population in countries with weak property rights. In countries that protect property rights, 93 percent of the population also has access to sewage treatment. But in countries that don't, the figure is only 48 percent. Norton found a similar correlation with life expectancy. He found that life expectancy is seventy years in countries with strong protection of property rights but only fifty years where property rights are only weakly protected. . . .

Part of the Mainstream

Aided by evidence such as this, free-market environmentalism has increasingly become part of the mainstream. Yes, there are still holdouts—economists who minimize the power of private property rights to protect the environment or who still believe that government can effectively correct problems in the marketplace. But these dwindle in number with each passing day. Indeed, five of the Nobel Prizes in economics awarded in the 1990s went to economists associated with the University of Chicago, the school of Friedman and other market-oriented scholars such as George Stigler.

Lester Thurow was right when he said in 1980 that environmental goods are an economic good like other consumer goods, but wrong when he said that they must be provided collectively. With property rights in place, markets are capable of supplying these goods just as readily as they do food. More than ever before, mainstream economists recognize this fact.

"I can find no basis for . . . [the belief] that we will have cleaner air and water and better protection for endangered species if the market runs the show."

Free-Market Principles Should Not Guide Environmental Policy

Carol Estes

Carol Estes is a freelance writer who frequently covers ecological issues. In the following viewpoint, she describes attending a conference sponsored by the Political Economy Research Center in which free-market approaches to conservation and environmental protection were discussed. Estes expresses doubts on whether the free market can be trusted to preserve America's environment and natural resources, arguing that too often in the past property owners have degraded the environment in the pursuit of short-term gains. Those who advocate market reforms also overlook how important government regulations have been in reducing pollution and protecting national parks, she asserts.

As you read, consider the following questions:

1. What value does Estes attach to property rights?
2. How might privatizing natural resources such as parks worsen the divide between the nation's rich and poor, according to the author?
3. What values besides economic ones should govern land management decisions, according to Estes?

Reprinted from Carol Estes, "Trading Park Futures," *National Parks*, September/October 1996. Copyright © 2000 National Parks Conservation Association. Reprinted with permission from the National Parks Conservation Association.

It is an October morning at the Mountain Sky Guest Ranch near Bozeman, Montana. The cold air smells of pine, and steam rises from a hot tub with a view of snow-covered peaks across the valley This is an exclusive place, $2,000 a week per person, where I cannot afford to vacation.

But I am not paying for this trip. This one is on PERC—the Political Economy Research Center—a conservative think tank that works out the economic theory behind the property rights movement. PERC has paid airfare, food, and lodging for most of the 20 journalists attending its New Shades of Green conference to hear about market solutions to environmental problems. The "product" PERC is selling during the next three days is something called "free market environmentalism." In the past five years, PERC has had more than 100 such conferences, casting a wide net of influence on journalists, academics, and congressional staffers.

What am I, an environmentalist, doing here? Environmentalism has lost its way, and I am here to find out why. I am here to rethink assumptions and to consider new answers; and because I love our public lands, and I am afraid we are losing them.

PERC has played fair in arranging the program. On the left are Kathryn Hohmann, director of environmental quality for the Sierra Club, and Brock Evans, National Audubon's vice president for national issues. On the far right is Chuck Cushman, founder of the National Inholder's Association, which is now the American Property Rights Association. His job at the conference, he tells me, is to "shake things up."

With the property rights association on the right and Audubon and Sierra on the left, PERC has placed itself strategically in what appears to be the rational middle. Our discussions begin from the premise that people are economic entities, motivated by financial self-interest. But the Perkies, as they call themselves, love nature, wildlife, clean water and air. They just claim they have found a way for us to have our environmental cake and eat it too.

PERC would first privatize public land. (All of it? They would not say.) Supposedly, this would be good for the environment because private owners have an economic incentive to take care of their land, which government does not. It would also lead to more efficient use of resources. What is wrong with the Perkies putting most of their eggs in the private property basket? In a way, nothing. I, for one, cherish the rights that go with my own .9 acres of Minnesota hillside—the right to be compensated if the government takes my property, and the right to exclude others. These rights are hard won, fought for since the 10th century, articulated in the Magna Carta, and codified in the Fifth Amendment of our Constitution. Property rights are a cornerstone of the American democratic system.

A Mystical Faith in Markets

However, PERC's arguments reveal an almost mystical faith in the market. Allocate resources to those who will use them wisely by making a profit, and those resources will live forever.

History tells a different story. People act in their own interest—usually the short-term profit kind. As [political journalist] E.J. Dionne says: "A capitalist society depends on noncapitalist values . . . to hold together and prosper." The free marketeers ignore the fact that a successful market society is "built on an older moral logic that predates capitalism."

Every enterprise—and everything is an enterprise in free market environmentalism—must pay its own way. Since recreation is the most highly subsidized of all the uses of public lands, recreational users, says PERC's executive director Terry Anderson, are "the biggest pigs at the trough." So national parks must be made to support themselves through user fees. If they cannot, then the sound of park gates closing is the sound of the market telling us we have too many parks.

They are right about one thing—recreational users should pay more. A visit to a national park costs less than two movie tickets. But they are also mixing apples and pine cones. Recreationists use public lands in a renewable way, as members of a nonexclusive club—U.S. taxpayers. Other subsidized users, miners and ranchers who often pay a fraction of market value for the right to use public land, use public resources for their own profit.

PERC also wants to get rid of "burdensome" environmental laws and regulations. These handcuff the market, halting or slowing economic activity that could create wealth and jobs that would, in turn, protect the environment. And besides, regulations are expensive, and they do not work.

No doubt these charges are true—some of the time. But the property rights folks sidestep the debate by ignoring the undeniable improvement in the environment since laws such as the Clean Air and Clean Water acts were passed in the early 1970s. Maybe it is time to look at new approaches; perhaps the market can be an important factor in protecting the environment. But unless we acknowledge the successes of the regulatory approach, along with its shortcomings, we are ignoring hard-won knowledge of what does work. Let's remember that these laws came into existence after our last bout with unregulated industry, because Americans were disgusted by sights such as the [polluted] Cuyahoga River in flames and human excrement floating in Lake Erie.

Mickey Siporin. Copyright © 1992 Mickey Siporin. Reprinted with permission.

PERC advocates the carrot of economic incentives in place of the stick of regulation. Rather than penalize people for violating the Endangered Species Act (ESA), free market environmentalists would pay them to comply. Under the current system, a rancher who finds wolves denning on his property might be tempted to kill them to protect his stock and avoid the federal interference triggered by the ESA. Free market environmentalists would pay him to let the wolves stay. Fair enough— pay to cover legitimate losses—if there are any. But can we really afford to start paying people to do the right thing?

Profit and Loss

Even if I think about free market environmentalism in terms of profit and loss, I find it disturbing. Bottom line, who will profit? The individuals and corporations with the wealth to buy up big tracts of federal land. And when we make that exchange, we trade the rights and privileges of millions of people, including future generations, for the rights of a single individual. After all, the real "little guy" is not a rancher or lumber company. He is someone who owns a home, or maybe no property at all. He will find himself locked out of lands that used to be his. Private Property, No Trespassing. In a country where the growing gulf between rich and poor worries even conservatives such as Pat Buchanan, how can another break for the rich make sense?

Who will profit by relaxing environmental laws? Polluters, certainly. But maybe businesses weighed down by too much paperwork will also be better off. Maybe enough jobs will be created to outweigh the many that will be lost. Even so, despite arguments, I can find no basis for PERC's faith that we will have cleaner air and water and better protection for endangered species if the market runs the show—even if we bid for the landowner's self-interest with our dwindling public funds.

Whether we like it or not, the national environmental discussion is turning in PERC's direction. When we enter these discussions, we cannot forget that the national parks, forests, grasslands, seashores are not "federal land." They are our land, yours and mine. If we lose them, we will never get them back. We must also remember that government is not bureaucrats. Government is us, and that simple notion is the foundation of democracy.

Let's refuse to base our policy decisions on economics alone. Fifty years ago, [ecologist] Aldo Leopold gave us a better standard: "Quit thinking about decent land-use as solely an economic problem. A thing is right when it tends to preserve the integrity, stability, and beauty of the biotic community. It is wrong when it tends otherwise."

"Industrialism, *the ethos encapsulating the values and technologies of Western civilization, is seriously endangering stable . . . environmental existence on this planet.*"

Technology and Modern Industry Must Be Rejected to Save the Environment

Kirkpatrick Sale

In the early 1800s, a group of British workers led by Ned Ludd destroyed and sabotaged machinery that they believed was taking away their jobs and livelihoods. The term "Luddite" came to mean someone opposed to industrialization and technological change. Social activist and author Kirkpatrick Sale examined the Luddite movement in his book *Rebels Against the Future: The Luddites and Their War on the Industrial Revolution: Lessons for the Machine Age.* In the following viewpoint, an article adaptation of that book, Sale argues that the spirit of the Luddites lives on in the writings of many ecological philosophers and activists who believe that technology and modern industrial society are destroying nature and impoverishing many humans. The Luddites and their philosophical successors offer important lessons concerning the future of modern society and on how the earth's biosphere can be preserved through the creation of sustainable human communities, Sale concludes.

As you read, consider the following questions:
1. Who are today's Luddites, according to Sale?
2. What seven lessons does Sale believe can be learned by studying the history of the Luddite movement?

We in the industrial world are in the middle of a social and political revolution that is almost without parallel. Call it "third wave" capitalism, or "postmodern," or "multi-national," or whatever; this transformation is, without anyone being prepared for it, overwhelming the communities and institutions and customs that once were the familiar stanchions of our lives. As *Newsweek* said, in a special issue that actually seemed to be celebrating it, this revolution is "outstripping our capacity to cope, antiquating our laws, transforming our mores, reshuffling our economy, reordering our priorities, redefining our workplaces, putting our Constitution to the fire, shifting our concept of reality."

No wonder there are some people who are Just Saying No.

They have a great variety of stances and tactics, but the technophobes and techno-resisters out there are increasingly coming together under the banner that dates to those attackers of technology of two centuries ago, the Luddites. In the past decade or so they have dared to speak up, to criticize this face of high technology or that, to organize and march and sue and write and propound, and to challenge the consequences as well as the assumptions of this second Industrial Revolution, just as the Luddites challenged the first. Some are even using similar strategies of sabotage and violence to make their point.

These neo-Luddites are more numerous today than one might assume, techno-pessimists without the power and access of the techno-optimists but still with a not-insignificant voice, shelves of books and documents and reports, and increasing numbers of followers—maybe a quarter of the adult population, according to a *Newsweek* survey. They are to be found on the radical and direct-action side of environmentalism, particularly in the American West; they are on the dissenting edges of academic economics and ecology departments, generally of the no-growth school; they are everywhere in Indian Country throughout the Americas, representing a traditional biocentrism against the anthropocentric norm; they are activists fighting against nuclear power, irradiated food, clear-cutting, animal experiments, toxic waste and the killing of whales, among the many aspects of the high-tech onslaught.

They may also number—certainly they speak for—some of those whose experience with modern technology has in one way or another awakened them from what [social critic] Lewis Mumford called "the myth of the machine." These would include those several million people in all the industrial nations whose jobs have simply been automated out from under them or have been sent overseas as part of the multinationals' global network, itself built on high-tech communications. They would include the many millions who have suffered from some exposure, officially sanctioned, to pollutants and poisons, medicines and chemicals, and live with the terrible results. . . .

The Price of Industrial Technology

Wherever the neo-Luddites may be found, they are attempting to bear witness to the secret little truth that lies at the heart of the modern experience: Whatever its presumed benefits, of speed or ease or power or wealth, industrial technology comes at a price, and in the contemporary world that price is ever rising and ever threatening. Indeed, inasmuch as industrialism is inevitably and inherently disregardful of the collective human fate and of the earth from which it extracts all its wealth—these are, after all, in capitalist theory "externalities"—it seems ever more certain to end in paroxysms of economic inequity and social upheaval, if not in the degradation and exhaustion of the biosphere itself.

From a long study of the original Luddites, I have concluded that there is much in their experience that can be important for the neo-Luddites today to understand, as distant and as different as their times were from ours. Because just as the second Industrial Revolution has its roots quite specifically in the first—the machines may change, but their *machineness* does not—so those today who are moved in some measure to resist (or who even hope to reverse) the tide of industrialism might find their most useful analogues, if not their models exactly, in those Luddites of the nineteenth century.

And as I see it, there are seven lessons that one might, with the focused lens of history, take from the Luddite past.

1. Technologies are never neutral, and some are hurtful. It was not all machinery that the Luddites opposed, but "all Machinery hurtful to Commonality," as a March 1812 letter to a hated manufacturer put it—machinery to which their commonality did not give approval, over which it had no control, and the use of which was detrimental to its interests, considered either as a body of workers or a body of families and neighbors and citizens.

Bioregionalism

Conservation biology, deep ecology, and other new disciplines are given a community constituency and real grounding by the bioregional movement. Bioregionalism calls for commitment to this continent *place by place*, in terms of biogeographical regions and watersheds. It calls us to see our country in terms of its landforms, plant life, weather patterns, and seasonal changes—its whole natural history before the net of political jurisdictions was cast over it. People are challenged to become "reinhabitory"—that is, to become people who are learning to live and think "as if" they were totally engaged with their place for the long future. This doesn't mean some return to a primitive lifestyle or utopian provincialism; it simply implies an engagement with community and a search for the sustainable sophisticated mix of economic practices that would enable people to live regionally and yet learn from and contribute to a planetary society.

Gary Snyder, *A Place in Space*, 1995.

What was true of the technology of industrialism at the beginning, when the apologist Andrew Ure praised a new machine that replaced high-paid workmen—"This invention confirms the great doctrine already propounded, that when capital enlists science in her service, the refractory hand of labour will always be taught docility"—is as true today, when a reporter for *Automation* could praise a computer system because it assures that "decision-making" is "removed from the operator . . . [and] gives maximum control of the machine to management." These are not accidental, ancillary attributes of the machines that are chosen; they are intrinsic and ineluctable.

Tools come with a prior history built in, expressing the values of a particular culture. A conquering, violent culture—of which Western civilization is a prime example, with the United States at its extreme—is bound to produce conquering, violent tools. When U.S. industrialism turned to agriculture after World War II, for example, it went at it with all that it had just learned on the battlefield, using tractors modeled on wartime tanks to cut up vast fields, crop-dusters modeled on wartime planes to spray poisons, and pesticides and herbicides developed from wartime chemical weapons and defoliants to destroy unwanted species. It was a war on the land, sweeping and sophisticated as modern mechanization can be, capable of depleting topsoil at the rate of 3 billion tons a year and water at the rate of 10 billion gallons a year. It could be no other way: If a nation like this beats its swords into plowshares, they will still be violent and deadly tools.

2. *Industrialism is always a cataclysmic process, destroying the past, roiling the present, making the future uncertain.* It is in the nature of the industrial ethos to value growth and production, speed and novelty, power and manipulation, all of which are bound to cause continuing, rapid and disruptive changes at all levels to society, and with some regularity, whatever benefits they may bring to a few. And because its criteria are essentially economic rather than, say, social or civic, those changes come about without much regard for any but purely materialist consequences and primarily for the aggrandizement of those few.

Whatever material benefits industrialism may introduce, the familiar evils—incoherent metropolises, spreading slums, crime and prostitution, inflation, corruption, pollution, cancer and heart disease, stress, anomie, alcoholism—almost always follow. . . .

3. *"Only a people serving an apprenticeship to nature can be trusted with machines."* This wise maxim of Herbert Read is what Wordsworth and the other Romantic poets of the Luddite era expressed in their own way as they saw the Satanic mills and Stygian forges both imprisoning and impoverishing textile families and usurping and befouling natural landscapes—"such outrage done to nature as compels the indignant power . . . to avenge her violated rights," as Wordsworth said.

What happens when an economy is not embedded in a due regard for the natural world, understanding and coping with the full range of its consequences to species and their ecosystems, is not only that it wreaks its harm throughout the biosphere in indiscriminate and ultimately unsustainable ways, though that is bad enough. It also loses its sense of the human as a species and the individual as an animal, needing certain basic physical elements for successful survival, including land and air, decent food and shelter, intact communities and nurturing families, without which it will perish as miserably as a fish out of water, a wolf in a trap. An economy without any kind of ecological grounding will be as disregardful of the human members as of the nonhuman, and its social as well as economic forms—factories, tenements, cities, hierarchies—will reflect that.

4. *The nation-state, synergistically intertwined with industrialism, will always come to its aid and defense, making revolt futile and reform ineffectual.* When the British government dispatched some 14,000 soldiers to put down the uprising of the Luddites in 1811 and 1812—a force seven times as large as any ever sent to maintain peace in England—it was sending a sharp signal of its inevitable alliance with the forces of the new industrialism. And it was not above cementing that alliance, despite all its talk of the rights of free Englishmen, with spies and informers, midnight raids, illegal arrests, overzealous magistrates and rigged trials, in aid of making the populace into a docile work force. That more than anything else established what a "laissez-faire" economy would mean—repression would be used by the state to insure that manufacturers would be free to do what they wished, especially with labor.

Since then, of course, the industrial regime has only gotten stronger, proving itself the most efficient and potent system for material aggrandizement the world has ever known, and all the while it has had the power of the dominant nation-states behind it, extending it to every corner of the earth and defending it once there. . . .

Resistance to the Industrial System

5. *But resistance to the industrial system, based on some grasp of moral principles and rooted in some sense of moral revulsion, is not only possible but necessary.* It is true that in a general sense the

Luddites were not successful either in the short-run aim of halting the detestable machinery or in the long-run task of stopping the Industrial Revolution and its multiple miseries; but that hardly matters in the retrospect of history, for what they are remembered for is that they *resisted*, not that they won. Some may call it foolish resistance ("blind" and "senseless" are the usual adjectives), but it was dramatic, forceful, honorable and authentic enough to have put the Luddites' issues forever on record and made the Luddites' name as indelibly a part of the language as the Puritans'.

What remains then, after so many of the details fade, is the sense of Luddism as a moral challenge, "a sort of moral earthquake," as Charlotte Brontë saw it in *Shirley*—the acting out of a genuinely felt perception of right and wrong that went down deep in the English soul. Such a challenge is mounted against large enemies and powerful forces not because there is any certainty of triumph but because somewhere in the blood, in the place inside where pain and fear and anger intersect, one is finally moved to refusal and defiance: "No more."

The ways of resisting the industrial monoculture can be as myriad as the machines against which they are aimed and as varied as the individuals carrying them out, as the many neo-Luddite manifestations around the world make clear. Some degree of withdrawal and detachment has also taken place, not alone among neo-Luddites, and there is a substantial "counterculture" of those who have taken to living simply, working in community, going back to the land, developing alternative technologies, dropping out or in general trying to create a life that does not do violence to their ethical principles.

The most successful and evident models for withdrawal today, however, are not individual but collective, most notably, at least in the United States, the Old Order Amish communities from Pennsylvania to Iowa and the traditional Indian communities found on many reservations across the country.

For more than three centuries now the Amish have withdrawn to islands mostly impervious to the industrial culture, and very successfully, too, as their lush fields, busy villages, neat farmsteads, fertile groves and gardens, and general lack of crime, poverty, anomie and alienation attest. In Indian country, too, where (despite the casino lure) the traditional customs and lifeways have remained more or less intact for centuries, a majority have always chosen to turn their backs on the industrial world and most of its attendant technologies, and they have been joined by a younger generation reasserting and in some cases revivifying those ancient tribal cultures. There could hardly be two systems more antithetical to the industrial—they are, for example, stable, communal, spiritual, participatory, oral, slow, cooperative, decentralized, animistic and biocentric—but the fact that such tribal societies have survived for so many eons, not just in North America but on every other continent as well, suggests that there is a cohesion and strength to them that is certainly more durable and likely more harmonious than anything industrialism has so far achieved.

6. *Politically, resistance to industrialism must force the viability of industrial society into public consciousness and debate.* If in the long run the primary success of the Luddite revolt was that it put what was called "the machine question" before the British public during the first half of the nineteenth century—and then by reputation kept it alive right into the twentieth—it could also be said that its failure was that it did not spark a true debate on that issue or even put forth the terms in which such a debate might be waged. That was a failure for which the Luddites of course cannot be blamed, since it was never part of their perceived mission to make their grievance a matter of debate, and indeed they chose machine-breaking exactly to push the issue beyond debate. But because of that failure, and the inability of subsequent critics of technology to penetrate the complacency of its beneficiaries and their chosen theorists, or to successfully call its values into question, the principles and goals of industrialism, to say nothing of the machines that embody them, have pretty much gone unchallenged in the public arena. Industrial civilization is today the water we swim in, and we seem almost as incapable of imagining what an alternative might look like, or even realizing that an alternative could exist, as fish in the ocean.

The political task of "resistance" today, then—beyond the "quiet acts" of personal withdrawal Mumford urged—is to try to make the culture of industrialism and its assumptions less invisible and to put the issue of its technology on the political agenda. . . . This means laying out as clearly and as fully as possible the costs and consequences of our technologies, in the near term and long, so that even those overwhelmed by the ease/comfort/speed/power of high-tech gadgetry (what Mumford called technical "bribery") are forced to understand at what price it all comes and who is paying for it. What purpose does this machine serve? What problem has become so great that it needs this solution? . . . Will this invention concentrate or disperse power, encourage or discourage self-worth? Can society at large afford it? Can the biosphere?

7. *Philosophically, resistance to industrialism must be embedded in an analysis—an ideology, perhaps—that is morally informed, carefully articulated and widely shared.* One of the failures of Luddism (if at first perhaps one of its strengths) was its formlessness, its unintentionality, its indistinctness about goals, desires, possibilities. If it is to be anything more than sporadic and martyristic, resistance could learn from the Luddite experience at least how important it is to work out some common analysis that is morally clear about the problematic present and the desirable future, and the common strategies that stem from it.

New Values

All the elements of such an analysis, it seems to me, are in existence, scattered and still needing refinement, perhaps, but there: in Mumford and E.F. Schumacher (*Small is Beautiful*) and Wendell Berry (*The Unsettling of America*) and Jerry Mander (*In the Absence of the Sacred*) and the Chellis Glendinning manifesto (*Utne Reader*, March/April 1990); in the writing of the Earth First!ers and the bioregionalists and deep ecologists; in the lessons and models of the Amish and the Iroquois; in the wisdom of tribal elders and the legacy of tribal experience everywhere; in the work of the long line of dissenters-from-progress and naysayers-to-technology. I think we might even be able to identify some essentials of that analysis, such as:

Industrialism, the ethos encapsulating the values and technologies of Western civilization, is seriously endangering

174

stable social and environmental existence on this planet, to which must be opposed the values and techniques of an organic ethos that seeks to preserve the integrity, stability and harmony of the biotic communities, and the human community within it.

Anthropocentrism, and its expression in both humanism and monotheism, is the ruling principle of that civilization, to which must be opposed the principle of biocentrism and the spiritual identification of the human with all living species and systems.

Globalism, and its economic and military expression, is the guiding strategy of that civilization, to which must be opposed the strategy of localism, based upon the empowerment of the coherent bioregion and the small community.

Industrial capitalism, as an economy built upon the exploitation and degradation of the earth, is the productive and distributive enterprise of that civilization, to which must be opposed the practices of an ecological and sustainable economy built upon accommodation and commitment to the earth and following principles of conservation, stability, self-sufficiency and cooperation.

"Some technologies are and will always be central to environmental protection."

Technology and Modern Industry Must Be Used to Preserve the Environment

Walter Truett Anderson

In the following viewpoint, Walter Truett Anderson argues that the future of environmental protection does not lie with those who reject modern technologies and industries, but instead with those who use them to actively manage ecosystems. Urging or coercing people simply to go "back to nature" is unrealistic and will do little for the environment, he asserts. Moreover, such a move fails to account for a world growing more industrialized, urbanized, and more technological every passing year. The conservation of natural resources and the preservation (and restoration) of relatively wild habitats require proactive human management using technology. Anderson is the author of several books including *Evolution Isn't What It Used to Be* and *The Future of the Self: Inventing the Postmodern Person.*

As you read, consider the following questions:

1. Who are the advocates of "back-to-nature environmentalism" according to Anderson?
2. What examples does the author give of how active human management has improved natural environments?
3. What argument does Anderson make about technology in general?

Some futurists say we are entering the "environmental century," and this will probably turn out to be right for a lot of reasons—some good and some bad. The good news is, more and more people are beginning to understand that a healthy environment is essential to everything we do. The bad news is, we're likely to have an ample enough supply of nasty problems to keep the environment on everybody's mind for a long time to come.

This doesn't mean the future is going to be terrible—far from it. It only means that there will be tough challenges, things for people and societies to work on and learn about. And it doesn't mean, either, that environmentalism—at least all the varieties of it that we hear about today—will be a potent force in this global civilization. Don't look for a great surge toward Green parties, or a worldwide burst of enthusiasm for deep ecology or bioregionalism. That back-to-nature sort of environmentalism seems to be enjoying a certain vogue at the moment, but actually the future will likely belong to what I call proactive environmentalists—people who are able to use information and technology, who don't mind living in this world as it is, and who are unafraid to engage in the hands-on management of ecosystems.

It's really amazing—especially in a society said to have reached the end of ideology almost 40 years ago—that the various strains of back-to-nature environmentalism such as deep ecology, bioregionalism, ecofeminism, and neo-Luddism have congealed so quickly into what any student of politics would recognize immediately as another ideology. It certainly has all the earmarks of one—a philosophy, a political movement, and enough jargon to gag a Washington speech-writer. Its dogma includes opposition to "anthropocentric"—i.e., human-centered—thought or action, a hands-off approach to nature, a deep suspicion of all things technological, a passion for the primitive, and a desire to get back to some kind of decentralized world in which people live and work within their bioregions, preferably with native plants and animals.

Hankering for the Past

This hankering for the past is one of the chief badges of membership in the movement. Some Americans—such as farmer-

177

author Wendell Berry—merely want to get back to the agricultural lifestyles of a few decades past, before the midcentury wave of mechanization. Many European Greens revere the medieval era. The real high rollers scorn agriculture altogether and yearn for the good old life of hunting and gathering. This last position was eloquently expressed by a former *Earth First! Journal* editor who wrote that "many of us . . . would like to see human beings live much more the way they did 15,000 years ago. . . ." Such ideas as these are remarkably popular on the campuses and in the coffee shops—and remarkably irrelevant to most of the valuable environmental work that is being done now and will be done in the future.

And that's the problem: The world is changing very quickly, and we desperately need a vision that engages this new world honestly and creatively, with daring and hope and perhaps even a touch of optimism. The appealing fantasies of back-to-nature environmentalism have the same effect on public dialogue that Gresham's law has on the economy. Bad money drives out good, and muzzy slogans drown out serious thinking. We simply are not in, nor about to be in, a world that resembles the bioregionalist dream of a small human population, most folks happily living simple lives in the country and leaving nature alone. It might be nice if we were, or it might not. But that really doesn't matter, because events aren't headed in that direction. The world is becoming more densely populated, not less; more urbanized, not less; more technological, not less. Most important of all, human beings are exerting ever more—not less—power in nature, having a greater impact on ecosystems. This is our world, and this is our work.

Proactive Environmentalism

The idea that people should somehow learn to "leave nature alone" has an aura of commendable humility, and it's the easiest thing imaginable to put into words, but it's quite impossible to put into practice in today's world. Proactive environmentalism—which deserves greater support and understanding from progressives—involves managing ecosystems, sometimes in ways that totally transform them. Every ecosystem, every population of wild animals, is, in one way or another, managed by human beings right now. Sure, there are different kinds of management, some of them trying to keep ecosystems relatively pristine and protect wildlife. But everywhere conservation is an active business that involves much more than merely battling exploitation. It also involves understanding information, using technology, and often making decisions that change ecosystems and affect the evolutionary future of species.

Restoration is one of the most important pieces of the new environmentalism. People are rebuilding rivers and streams and ponds and beaches, reconstructing forests and prairies and deserts, sometimes coaxing populations of near-extinct species back to a sustainable size. I don't know whether to call ecological restoration an art or a science or a technology, because it's a bit of all those; but it's sure as hell not a matter of leaving nature alone. In most places, certainly in the more developed parts of the world, you don't get a restored ecosystem by fencing it off and doing nothing. Do that, and the result will be a lot of native plants and animals coexisting more or less peacefully with a lot of nonnative ones. Many such mixed ecosystems can be found in national, state, and regional parks, and in the privately held rural areas that are not-too-accurately called "nature preserves." And there's nothing wrong with that; they maintain open space, habitat, and watershed, and they're valuable and beautiful and productive in many ways.

But a true restoration project—like the piece of American prairie that the great naturalist Aldo Leopold and his associates began carving out of a Wisconsin cornfield about 60 years ago—is a deliberate human creation. Those pioneer restorationists hauled in tons of soil, ripped out everything that didn't have proof of citizenship, and planted thousands of native seeds and seedlings they had found in various places more or less close to the site. Nowadays we have lots of small restoration projects, even in urban areas. Volunteers in Marin County, near San Francisco, pitch in to restore local salmon streams where construction work and erosion from neighboring pastures have ruined spawning beds. Work crews spend their weekends making small check dams on the tributaries to prevent sediment from spilling into the creeks, wrestling rocks into place along the cattle-damaged banks, and rebuilding the spawning areas.

You can also find similar projects undertaken on a larger scale by professional restorationists such as the "river doctors" who work in places like Washington and Montana and Colorado, bringing back streams that have suffered badly at the hands (and feet) of miners, cattle herds, and developers.

Larger yet is the project to repair the Florida Everglades, which—if it's carried out as currently proposed—will be the largest water-system restoration in history. Most of the work will be done by the U.S. Army Corps of Engineers, which in the past has taken a beating from environmental writers, myself included. But the corps' mind-set is changing. Instead of master-planning everything, the restorers are using what they call "adaptive management," which means proceeding with a general objective, trying some things (different ways of modifying levees, for example), and seeing what works best. It's a pragmatic and flexible approach that, while far from "hands-off" restoration, certainly isn't the same as the heavy-handed replumbing of ecosystems so often practiced in the past.

The Everglades are not, of course, going to be restored to what they were a few hundred years ago—not in southern Florida with its enormous agricultural areas, its cities with millions of inhabitants, and God knows how many tourists coming to fish and take romantic boat rides through the sloughs. But restorations—even "true restorations" like the Wisconsin prairie—are never perfect reproductions of a past ecosystem. They are different because of what's not there—species that have become extinct—and also because of what *is* there: Inevitably, some bird, insect, or plant newcomer succeeds in sneaking in and making itself at home. Also, the restorationist always has to make a choice about what past state to emulate. The image of homeostasis—like much of the rest of the pop ecology that informs the back-to-nature mystique—is inaccurate. "Undisturbed" ecosystems change too, sometimes dramatically, and any restoration project mimics a certain era, much as an "old town" mimics a certain stage in a city's history. You have to decide what nature to go back to—which is yet another way of saying you can't get away from human agency. Furthermore, restored ecosystems don't stay restored unless somebody puts in a lot of work keeping them that way.

A restoration project, then, is a technique of environmental management in the present and not a return to the past. Some restoration projects are about improving the depleted soil of farmlands. Some are about restoring populations of certain plant or animal species, like the controversial return of the wolves now roaming in and around Yellowstone National Park. Others—like Holistic Resource Management (HRM), which includes a style of cattle ranching being tried out in many parts of the American West—are essentially techniques for using natural resources without using them up.

Dangerous Luddites

The real beliefs of the greens do not appear in the major media. We are told that they are our environmental leaders— but they are not environmentalists at all; they are Luddites. They are in the tradition of Ned Ludd, who from 1811– 1816, tried to reverse the course of industrialization by smashing machinery. Ludd thought that industrialization was costing jobs. The current breed of Luddites is far more dangerous because they have enormous political power and wealth, and they operate behind a fog created by a cooperative media. . . .

A major characteristic of Luddites is that they stubbornly refuse to acknowledge the environmental gains they see around them. Thus, they cannot learn from history. Try to find in Al Gore's *Earth in the Balance* any mention of America's increased forests, wildlife and biodiversity or our reduced erosion. Yet Virginia, adjacent to Washington, D.C., and Gore's beautiful home state of Tennessee, are classic examples of great changes that have occurred.

James Dunn, *21st Century*, Winter 1998–1999.

HRM ranching begins with the somewhat startling proposition that grasslands should be periodically trampled down and fertilized by big herds of hoofed animals—as they once were by buffalo and elk. This breaks up hard crusts, keeps the soil porous and receptive to rain, helps decompose dried grass stalks and other such materials, and works minerals into the soil. The tricky part is that buffalo herds moved around, whereas most cattle herds stay in one place, overgraze, and produce erosion. The "holistic" solution is to simulate the behavior of the long-gone native herds by bunching the grazing animals together, letting them feed for a while in one place, then moving them and giving the just-grazed area an opportunity to recover. I'm not yet convinced that Holistic Resource Management is the solution to soil damage from cattle ranching, but at the very least it is turning out to be a peacemaker in the range wars between ranchers and environmentalists. And it may be the key to the large-scale restoration of bison populations in the American West.

In forestry, a lot of attention is being paid now to the "reactive" kind of environmentalism—stopping the clear-cutters, saving the rainforests—and those are indeed worthwhile and necessary efforts. But most of the effective forest protection today, and nearly all of the reforestation, is active management. Agroforestry—which means either growing trees as crops or integrating tree-growing into other crops—is essential. In Tanzania, where deforestation is so severe people have to travel miles to find wood, some farmers are using an agroforestry technology known as "rotational woodlots." They plant trees, mostly varieties of Australian acacia, alongside their regular food crops. The farmers continue to grow and harvest food for two or three years until the trees take over. Then the field becomes a woodlot and a source of fuelwood, poles for buildings, and fodder for animals—meanwhile restoring fertility to the soil like any fallow—until the farmers clear-cut it and go back to growing crops between the stumps.

In other parts of the world, farmers are planting the New Zealand-bred "super trees." These tall trees, sometimes called "kiwi willows," sprout like mad. They are grown for energy, fodder, or timber, and may help forests store carbon dioxide. Since they are hybrids, they're sterile and don't produce seeds that can escape and take over an ecosystem.

But bioregional purists don't like these kinds of agroforestry: Super trees are not exactly natural and Australian acacias don't ordinarily grow in Africa.

Some of the most interesting and really innovative projects going on now—like the coastal desert developments in which crops are irrigated with seawater—don't fit neatly into any category. They don't meet even the most spacious definition of restoration, because they thoroughly make over sizable pieces of real estate, turning them into ecosystems of a sort that never existed before.

Fly over the coastline of the Arabian Sea or the Gulf of California, and here and there you can look down and see seawater farms—green circles on the parched land. They are the advance guard of an entirely new kind of agriculture, now being developed by a team of scientists at Planetary Design Corp. in Arizona. CEO Carl Hodges and his associates studied hundreds of saltwater plants and then began to focus on salicornia, which grows along marshy coastlines and produces a crunchy, pleasant-tasting stalk—kind of like a lightly salted string bean. Salicornia, under various names, has been known as an edible plant for centuries—it was a favorite snack of George Washington—but was never bred or cultivated. The scientists began breeding new strains, hoping to get one that could produce high-quality oil and meal. Eventually they got two promising varieties. They plan to use salicornia not only for seawater-based food production, but also for soil-building, stimulating new urban development along coastal deserts, and taking carbon dioxide (CO_2) out of the atmosphere. Salicornia will be a piece, perhaps a small piece or perhaps a very large one, of the effort to feed the world during the next 50 years or so of continuing population growth. And it will also be a piece of the attempt to find methods of development that are not only locally sustainable, but active contributors to environmental management on a large—indeed, global—scale. Hodges calls it "climate defensive food production."

Salicornia farming is an excellent example of proactive environmentalism. First of all, it starts with recognizing and accepting the present and near-future global situation. The world in which the salicornia enthusiasts expect to do their work is not ecotopia. It is a densely populated, urbanizing, developing world with vast amounts of land already degraded by erosion, depleting freshwater supplies, and an ever-increasing need for fossil fuels.

Farming salicornia is not chemical intensive, because the seawater provides most of the nutrients needed for growing the crops, but otherwise it violates most of the ideals of small-scale bioregional agriculture: It's commercial farming; it needs a good-sized capital investment; it uses sophisticated irrigation technology; and it is based on a plant native to few of the places where the crops now grow.

Projects such as this inspire enthusiasm from most people—but are scornfully dismissed as "technological fixes" by back-to-nature true believers.

The term technological fix deserves some attention here, since it's one of the staples of ecotopian rhetoric, along with the promiscuous overuse—to the point of meaninglessness—of the word "natural." The argument against simply fixing up something with a technological repair job may well apply in some specific cases—if, for example, a person is presented with the choice between having a quadruple bypass and adopting a healthy lifestyle—but it really doesn't have much relevance to most current environmental concerns. The world is not faced with a simple choice of either adopting more environmentally sensitive attitudes or applying new technologies. Rather, we are seeing both a rapid evolution of technology away from heavy industrialism *and* value shifts about the environment.

Taking Ideas Too Far

Most of the other back-to-nature terms are similarly pumped-up and carelessly repeated concepts that have a certain amount of reasonableness if taken in moderation. That great favorite, "anthropocentrism," for example. This isn't just a challenge to the habit of valuing plants and animals only for their usefulness to humans—which is something that needs challenging. The self-described "deep ecologists" are not interested in any such sensible objective. They escalate the rhetoric and prescribe that human beings learn how to live in equality with all other living things. However charming this might sound, it has utterly nothing to do with a world that is about to have 6 billion people in it, whether we like it or not.

Bioregionalism, too, is a useful idea in some contexts—such as governance of air basins. But it becomes pure nonsense when people begin to advocate it—as Kirkpatrick Sale does in his book *Dwellers in the Land*—as a solution to be imposed on the whole world, by relocating people from the cities to rural areas where they would then take up ecologically correct lifestyles. There are indeed people who remain in one place, don't get hooked into the global economy, and rarely travel—all parts of the bioregional answer—and that's a perfectly fine way to live. The trouble is in turning it into a universal mandate and a political agenda—a crusade to get everybody living that way. Not everybody does, not everybody wants to, and not everybody can.

Even the people who talk bioregionalism don't live that way—and don't seem to notice the gap between what they say and how they live. Some years back, *Sierra* magazine ran an interview with poet Gary Snyder, in which he advised all of us: "Quit moving. Stay where you are . . . become a *paysan*, *paisano*, *peón*." He then proceeded directly, with no evident sense of irony, to telling of his recent trips to China and Alaska. A bit further on he added: "I've been traveling eight or 10 weeks a year, doing lectures and readings at universities and community centers around the United States. I'm able to keep a sense of what's going on in the country that way."

I don't think this makes Snyder a hypocrite. I think he's a perfectly honest guy who would rather recycle green platitudes for admiring listeners than think hard about what it really means to live in a global civilization.

Probably the most serious weakness of pop ecophilosophy is its Luddite tilt. Technology isn't just a thing—it is human thought, action, information, and invention, and a living part of who and what we are. Some applications of technology are lousy and some are wonderful. But simply taking sides for or against technology is the lowest common denominator of public discourse.

Information Technologies and the Environment

Some technologies are and will always be central to environmental protection. I doubt that most people realize how important information technologies are in environmental management today. We worry about the hole in the ozone layer—and we should worry about it—but don't appreciate the exquisite technology involved in detecting it, monitoring its ebbs and flows, projecting its future. Nobody *sees* a hole in the ozone. Like many other major environmental issues, it is accessible to our understanding only through the use of monitoring technologies.

An enormous environmental information system has grown, spreading and connecting around the world. The living Earth is now inseparable from this ever-expanding complex of satellites, transmitters, relay towers, computers, and software. With these devices, people observe the condition of the ozone, speculate on the future of the world's climate, study tectonic movements deep below the surface, brood over the oceans, track the migrations of wild animals and the changes in forests and deserts. This is technology that doesn't fit into any simplistic pro vs. con debate. It is neither the malevolent cause of our problems nor their magical solution—just an essential means of acquiring information. And it will play a larger part in bringing greater environmental awareness than the collected works of all the writers and philosophy professors who push deep ecology and bioregionalism.

So far most of the buzz about the "information revolution" has focused on its organizational, economic, and cultural impact, with far less attention paid to its biological side. It's high time we recognized that we are becoming not just an information society but a bioinformation society. And a global one. Ecological information will play a central role in everything people do in this society, and so will biotechnology. . . .

Dealing with Power

We are going forward into an interesting few decades. With a bit of wisdom and good will—not to mention luck—we will reach the latter part of the next century with population on the decline, new opportunities for restoration and ecosystem management, and a great tool kit of technology and bioinformation. But along the way, we will have to come to terms with power. The back-to-nature mystique is based on opposition to human power in nature, and its followers are always reluctant to acknowledge having any themselves. This pose has its advantages: If you say you don't have such power and don't want anybody else to have it, you both establish your own personal goodness and duck all the problems that come with having it. But the truth is that we all have a lot of power—both individually, and collectively as a species—and will have more as time goes on.

In his book *Power and Innocence*, Rollo May eloquently dissected the psychology of "pseudoinnocence"—a willful inability to deal maturely with power. "We cannot develop responsibility," he wrote, "for what we don't admit we have." He was talking about interpersonal relations, but the observation applies equally well to the larger human undertaking of learning our way into the 21st century. We have to admit to having power, face the impossibility of leaving nature alone, and cultivate our environmental ethics and policies accordingly. And as that happens, we may begin to develop some genuinely deep ecology.

"We must broaden our concept of national security to include the concepts of preventive defense and environmental security."

The United States Should Treat the Environment as a National Security Issue

William A. Nitze

William A. Nitze is an assistant administrator with the Environmental Protection Agency (EPA). In the following viewpoint, taken from a 1997 speech, he contends America must broaden its concept of national security to include the relatively new concept of "environmental security"—the recognition of the fact that international environmental and global resource problems have negative impacts on U.S. national interests. The EPA consequently has become a key player in U.S. foreign policy, he concludes.

As you read, consider the following questions:

1. What example does Nitze give of United States/Russian cooperation on the environment?
2. According to the author, what recommendation did the EPA Science Advisory Board make concerning national security?
3. What steps has the EPA taken in to coordinate with other federal agencies, according to Nitze?

Excerpted from William A. Nitze, "Environmental Security," speech to the World Affairs Council, January 16, 1997.

I want to talk about Environmental Protection Agency's (EPA) international role, and especially to highlight a new direction for EPA into the area of environmental security.

EPA is a key player in carrying out U.S. foreign policy. You may not be fully aware of the depth of our involvement in international activities. Let me begin with a story about radioactive waste in Russia.

Murmansk Project

At present [1997] Russia does not have adequate facilities to store nuclear materials from decommissioned submarines and has, until 1993, resorted to dumping both high- and low-level radioactive waste into the Arctic Seas and low-level waste into the Sea of Japan. Russia is currently storing spent and damaged nuclear fuel and other solid radioactive waste materials on ships and barges in the Arctic near Murmansk. Such floating storage facilities create significant risks of radioactive contamination of our environment.

The inability of Russia to manage its military nuclear waste (in both the Arctic and Far East) has prevented it from signing the London Convention, an international agreement that bans the dumping of all radioactive waste in the oceans. In addition, Russia has been unable to meet its submarine decommissioning goals under the START [Strategic Arms Reduction Talks] agreement due to inadequate liquid-radioactive waste processing capacity.

This problem has become urgent as an increasing number of nuclear submarines are being decommissioned. Waste from these subs is being temporarily stored on land and in floating vessels in the Murmansk region of the Kola Peninsula. Waste storage facilities are reported to be 90–95 percent full.

In 1993, the Russian Federation made it clear that if interested countries could assist them in solving this problem in both northwest Russia and the Far East, then Russia would be prepared to formally adhere to the ban under the London Convention.

In June 1994 under a U.S., Norway, and the Russian Federation initiative EPA began exploring the possibility of expanding and upgrading the only operational Russian low-level liquid radioactive waste processing facility. Located in Murmansk, this facility was designed to process the waste from Russia's nuclear powered icebreakers fleet.

The idea of upgrading the Murmansk facility was presented to the Gore-Chernomyrdin Commission in June of 1994 by EPA Administrator Carol Browner. Subsequently, on September 28, 1994, President Bill Clinton and [Russian president Boris] Yeltsin issued a joint U.S.-Russian Summit announcement stating that resolution of this liquid radioactive waste processing problem is an important component of efforts to protect Arctic environmental quality and natural resources. Today [January 16, 1997], construction has begun on the new facility; Russia has voluntarily refrained from ocean dumping; and President Yeltsin has indicated Russia's intent to sign the London Convention.

I tell this story because it illustrates, quite strikingly, how EPA can help achieve the U.S. government's international environmental objectives. This initiative was designed and implemented with EPA leadership. Our goal was to enhance U.S. environmental security by protecting the Arctic ecosystem and obtaining Russian compliance with an international treaty to protect the world's oceans.

EPA's International Role

Today EPA is interacting with dozens of governments around the world. EPA was and remains a key agency on the ground in Eastern Europe after the fall of communism. We opened the Regional Environmental Center in Budapest in 1990. For the past six years [since 1990] we have sent dozens of missions to countries of Eastern Europe to help them build their capability to deal with environmental problems.

What pleases me most about these activities is that we have had a real impact on improving the quality of life in Eastern Europe. The drinking water supply in Krakow is now safer because of an EPA program that supplied technical assistance and American disinfection equipment to that historic city in Poland. EPA air monitoring equipment and training played a critical role in reducing Krakow's air pollution by 50 percent since 1989. We have been doing the same in Russia and in many other countries.

EPA's expertise and experience in dealing with environmental problems are in great demand throughout the world, a demand that far exceeds our limited resources. We are therefore forced to make difficult decisions about where our modest resources will have the largest impact. These decisions are made more difficult by the need to broaden our work with foreign governments well beyond technical assistance. The interaction of environmental, trade and commercial interests in the world today require us to be an integral part of the development and implementation of foreign, trade and economic policies.

Environmental Security

My Murmansk story demonstrates a new dimension to EPA's international work—-the issue of environmental security. Environmental security is a relatively new concept in the language of international diplomacy. My colleagues in the State Department often refer to it as "environmental diplomacy." And in the Defense Department, alleviating environmental problems before they become cause for military conflict is part of [Defense] Secretary William Perry's concept of "Preventive Defense."

For EPA, environmental security is the minimization of environmental trends or conditions involving other countries that could, over time, have significant negative impacts on important U.S. national interests. Environmental security is the way that the U.S. will look at international environmental issues in the future. It is the way that our environmental activities abroad will serve our domestic responsibilities.

Political borders are not barriers to environmental problems. To protect the health of our citizens, the environment of the U.S. and our foreign policy interests, we must pay attention to what is happening to the environment on a regional and global scale. The potential radioactive pollution of the Arctic that I described above, climate change and ozone depletion are just the first three on what may become a long list of environment threats to the U.S. that need to be addressed internationally. Just as we have now integrated economics and trade into most aspects of U.S. foreign policy so must we broaden our concept of national security to include the concepts of preventive defense and environmental security if we are to succeed in protecting the long term health and quality of the life of the American people. In the years ahead, water quality and quantity may be one of the most important environmental and security issues.

For example, there are major river systems such as the Euphrates, where there is no existing international framework. In South Africa, five rivers flow into Mozambique without international controls. Growing water problems in the Middle East represent major security issues. EPA is working on these problems and is part of the Middle East Accord working group on the environment.

In 1996 the EPA Science Advisory Board completed a report entitled "Beyond the Horizon." This report urged EPA to think about future risks including threats to the environmental security of the United States and effective response strategies. The report said:

> EPA should begin working with relevant agencies and organizations to develop strategic national policies that link national security, foreign relations and environmental quality and economic growth.

The report called for an "early-warning" system to identify potential future environmental risks.

We have taken this recommendation seriously.

Since the end of the cold war, many parts of the world have seen marked improvements in human rights and the spread of democracy and free markets. People who were under totalitarian governments in the former Soviet Union and the countries in Central and Eastern Europe just six years ago are now more free to travel and pursue opportunity. The United States is more secure from military threats than anytime since before the Second World War.

Much has been written and said about the global economy and the need for America to take a global approach to business. Problems and opportunities in one region have immediate impacts in another. This globalization accompanied by unchecked population growth in much of the developing world will lead to greater competition for important natural resources and increase the world's capacity to damage the natural environment to a degree that is only now becoming frighteningly clear.

At the same time, regional instabilities, terrorism, and international organized crime are all problems that have grown worse since the cold war ended. The end of the cold war exposed and unleashed many regional problems that had been suppressed by U.S.-Soviet competition. The expanding global economy together with the population explosion have globalized the consequences of these problems. Greenhouse gases released in a rapidly growing Asia can change the world's [atmosphere], and nuclear accidents in Russia can affect the United States as we saw with the Chernobyl disaster. Reported cases of CFC [ozone-damaging chloroflurocarbons] smuggling from Russia into the U.S., chemical terrorism in Japan and desertification in Northern Mexico are but a few of the potential environmental threats around the world that we need to face now.

National Interests and the Environment

The environment has a profound impact on our national interests in two ways: First, environmental forces transcend borders and oceans to threaten directly the health, prosperity, and jobs of American citizens. Second, addressing national resources is frequently critical to achieving political and economic stability, and to pursuing our strategic goals around the world.

Warren Christopher, "American Diplomacy and the Global Environmental Challenges of the 21st Century," address at Stanford University, April 9, 1996.

Most governmental efforts to protect the environment are directed at problems of present conditions (e.g., emissions from industrial pollution) and legacies of past "solutions" (e.g., abandoned waste sites). With the notable exception of some major environmental treaties relatively little consideration is given to problems that may arise tomorrow. By explicitly considering the future today, we can make decisions about today's known environmental problems and avoid or manage tomorrow's unknown environmental problems so as to minimize future negative impacts.

In some few instances, the international community has

been effective in taking a collective long-range view; the Montreal Protocol which limits the production and use of chloroflurocarbons is an outstanding example. If similar technical foresight had been exercised during the early development and use of other materials such as polychlorinated biphenyls or PCBs, significant damage to human health and the environment and the expenditure of vast resources on a clean-up, could have been avoided.

These problems point to the need for EPA to play a large role in implementing U.S. Government foreign policy agenda.

The World Ahead

The Clinton Administration has already formally acknowledged the importance of environmental and natural resource issues for U.S. national security. In the 1996 document "A National Security Strategy of Engagement and Enlargement," the Administration noted that "Even when making the most generous allowance for advances in science and technology, one cannot help but conclude that population growth and environmental pressures will feed into immense social unrest and make the world *substantially more vulnerable to serious international frictions.*"

In a speech at Stanford University on April 9, 1996, U.S. Secretary of State Warren Christopher explicitly recognized the need to make environmental security a central dimension of U.S. foreign policy. He said that the environment has a profound impact on our national interests in two ways: first, environmental forces transcend borders and oceans to threaten directly the health, prosperity and jobs of American citizens. Second: addressing natural resource issues is frequently critical to achieving political and economic stability, and to pursuing our strategic goals around the world.

As I mentioned earlier, Dr. William Perry, the U.S. Secretary of Defense, has put forward the idea of preventive defense as a central precept of U.S. defense planning. Preventive defense implies that the U.S. military should not only anticipate and respond to threats to U.S. national security if and when they occur, but should play an active role in preventing those threats from arising in the first place. Although implementation plans have not been completed, the

U.S. military has made a commitment to minimize any negative environmental impacts of its own operations and to seek ways of improving environmental conditions in the areas where it carries out military and nonmilitary missions.

EPA is building new partnerships within the U.S. Government. Recognizing that no single agency can meet the challenges alone EPA has recently entered into a *Memorandum of Understanding* on environmental security with the Department of Defense and the Department of Energy. This agreement will allow the special expertise in each of the three organizations to be leveraged with support from the State Department and other agencies. The three partners will initially focus on projects in the Baltic countries, Eastern Europe and the countries of the former Soviet Union related to the environmental legacy of the Cold War.

Even before the development of this Memorandum of Understanding, EPA at the invitation of the Department of Defense began participating in the Arctic Military Environmental Cooperation (AMEC) process. AMEC is an outgrowth of the trilateral military discussions between the United States, Norway and Russia and is concerned with threats to the Arctic environment related to military-industrial activities in the Arctic region. Currently, EPA is developing a project under AMEC to design and build a transportable storage container to solve the interim storage problem of damaged and spent nuclear fuel from Russian submarines and icebreakers. The existing floating fuel storage situation is viewed by the three countries as posing a serious health and safety risk for the Arctic region.

At the request of the Panama Canal Commission, we will also begin training of Panamanians on hazardous waste management.

At the same time, EPA is now developing its own strategic plan for environmental security. Our program will draw heavily on EPA's core functions including emergency planning and response, environmental crimes investigation, environmental terrorism, technical assistance and training, hazardous waste management, and monitoring and risk assessment. It will have a new focus on "Futures Planning," including development of an early warning system.

New Challenges

I believe in the decade ahead that environmental issues will comprise a large and growing element of U.S. foreign policy. America will be faced with many more environmental and natural resource–based security challenges in the future. As a result, global environmental quality issues represent one of the single most important strategic issues that will face the U.S. at the dawn of a new century.

"The incursion of the military into environmental affairs is cause for great concern."

The United States Should Not Treat the Environment as an Issue of National Security

Paul Benjamin

The concept of environmental security became important in U.S. foreign policy in the 1990s under administration of President Bill Clinton and Vice President Al Gore, says Paul Benjamin in the following viewpoint. However, Benjamin argues that such a focus on the environment is harmful for several reasons. It could lead to military solutions to environmental problems and to confusion over what civilian and military agencies of the government should do. In addition, he contends that American efforts to dictate environmental policies to other nations may actually increase the possibility of conflict between nations and may involve the United States in wars that would themselves do great harm to the environment. Benjamin is an independent foreign policy analyst.

As you read, consider the following questions:

1. What future conflicts and wars does Benjamin speculate may happen if environmental security becomes a guiding focus of U.S. foreign policy?
2. What sort of forms can environmental security policies take, according to the author?
3. How might policies geared towards environmental security increase the chances of American involvement in wars, according to Benjamin?

In 2015 the United States invades Brazil to put an end to logging in the rainforests. In 2020 war breaks out in Western Africa as people vie for arable land in the face of a rapidly encroaching desert, and the United States and its NATO allies intervene to prevent a wider war. By 2022 the U.S. military is running domestic and overseas poverty reduction and population control schemes and dominates a global environmental surveillance network. Implausible? Not necessarily, if current trends in U.S. security policy continue unabated.

Since the collapse of the Soviet Union in 1991, policymakers have struggled to redefine the security interests of the United States. With the overriding threat of the previous half century no longer in existence, America has had to take a new look at where threats to its security may occur, and how best to deal with them. While debate rages over what to do about the proliferation of weapons of mass destruction, how to redefine America's strategic relationships, and whether we need a national missile defense system, more subtle changes in security policy thinking are taking place in the background.

The concept of security has been expanding gradually. In the past, "security," although never rigorously defined, in practice usually meant what Stephen Walt, in his classic definition, refers to as decisions involving "the threat, use, and control of military force." During the Cold War, that understanding of security led to a policy of containing the Soviet Union through nuclear and conventional deterrence strategies. In recent years, however, there has been a conscious shift from a limited, largely military, sense of "security" to one that encompasses all manner of "threats," ranging from environmental degradation to poverty and from overpopulation to ethnic tensions. New issues are continually being classified as security issues or threats to national security in what one commentator [Stephen Del Rosso] has referred to as "an additive 'laundry list' approach." The consequence is that a diverse set of new problems and goals is entering security discourse, and a whole range of social issues that were previously limited to the civilian sphere is increasingly falling under the purview of the U.S. military.

That development is troubling for numerous reasons. . . .

One of the major problems with redefining security so broadly as to include environmental issues is that it risks rendering the word "security" meaningless. As Daniel Deudney, a professor of international relations at Johns Hopkins University, has argued, "If everything that causes a decline in human well-being is labeled a 'security' threat, the term loses any analytical usefulness and becomes a loose synonym of 'bad.'" Clear language is essential for clear thinking, as George Orwell has persuasively argued. When "security" becomes ambiguous and diluted, two dangers become apparent.

First, there is a high risk that turning environmental issues into a security concern will result in the militarization of environmental policy, with detrimental effects on society and on efforts to find solutions to environmental problems. The second danger is that environmental security policies may actually reduce security—especially if they tend to push toward conflict rather than peaceful relations among nations. Before examining those issues, however, it is worth asking what policymakers and government agencies mean when they talk about "environmental security."

What Is Environmental Security?

Government agencies and officials rarely clarify their terms. The words "security" and "national interest" are bandied about with such frequency that it is often hard to challenge their usage and demand definitions. Nonetheless, it is possible to deduce certain linkages between environmental degradation and national security from the actions and words of the people involved. The key assumptions include the following:

- Environmental degradation and resource depletion threaten American health, prosperity, and lives and need to be countered.
- Poor environmental conditions and lack of resources will lead to regional instability and conflict, and the United States will then need to intervene.
- Environmental modification might be used as a weapon of war, and preparations should be made for such use.
- Environmental conditions affect the success of Wash-

ington's overseas military deployments and must be studied.

- Providing for America's defense should be done in an environmentally safe manner.

The 1999 *National Security Strategy* cites both environmental threats to human life and environmentally induced instability at a regional level as issues that compromise national security. While President Bill Clinton emphasizes the conflict model ("preserving the resources we share is crucial . . . to maintain *stability and peace within nations and among them*"), Vice President Al Gore opts for the health and prosperity approach, emphasizing the effect of the environment on the "quality of life.". . .

The Conflict Approach and the Well-Being Approach

The conflict model is best expressed by Thomas Homer-Dixon at the University of Toronto, although there is a significant body of other academic research on this subject.

Homer-Dixon's extensive studies on the relationship between acute environmental change and conflict have tested three hypotheses: (a) environmental scarcity causes simple-scarcity conflicts between states (so-called resource wars); (b) environmental scarcity causes large population movement, which in turn causes group-identity conflicts; and (c) environmental scarcity simultaneously increases economic deprivation and disrupts key social institutions, which in turn causes "deprivation" conflicts such as civil strife and insurgency. He concludes that evidence supporting the last two hypotheses is much stronger than that supporting the first, although the results from other academic research are more mixed.

Such clarity is sadly not to be found in the Clinton administration's rhetoric—the examples given earlier are as much as can be ascertained of the government's view of the link between the environment and instability. Instead, the administration has jumped in with two assumptions: first, that there is such a link and, second, that something can and should be done about it. . . .

The well-being approach to environmental security is

even less well defined than the conflict approach. Essentially, any environmental problem that in any way reduces the quality of life in America or affects the health of American citizens can be considered a threat to national security. This approach also allows any environmental policy and any environmental program, in the United States or overseas, to be considered in the national interest. Such a dilution of the concept of security has profound effects on the way that policy is elaborated and implemented, and it takes no account of tradeoffs between values.

New Goals, Confused Goals

Environmental security takes many forms. It includes carrying out defense activities in compliance with environmental standards, preparing for environmentally induced conflict overseas, cooperating with foreign militaries to tackle environmental issues, and developing policies and signing agreements on environmental issues such as climate change, air pollution, and toxic waste disposal. Each is a different issue, but there are some similarities. All are deemed to require immediate action. Such is the imperative of invoking "security," and thus its rhetorical value, as a motivating tool. All environmental security activities include some activity overseas as well as in the domestic sphere—to prevent conflict, to mitigate conflict, and to reduce threats to American life and living standards. In short, anything environmental is now considered a national security issue.

Subsuming all those goals under the title "environmental security" makes a muddled "catch-all" policy inevitable. It is worrisome when any environmental policy or project can be designated "in the national interest," and any environmental problem can be branded a "threat to national security." Those terms should not be taken lightly. They are mobilizing terms designed to prioritize projects; muddling the concept of security makes it easier to avoid providing a coherent rationale for them. That is not a trivial point. Several large "environmental national security" projects have already gone forward without a proper analysis of how they really affect national security, or even what is meant by the concept. That also is not a new problem. Arnold Wolfers recognized it when he wrote in 1962 that "the term 'security' covers a range of goals so wide that highly divergent policies can be interpreted as policies of security." However, instead of taking note of this caution, the new security policymakers and policy wonks continue to use the term "environmental security" with carefree abandon.

As a result, the term "security" is in serious danger of being appropriated by any cause that wishes to use it. This is not to assume that all causes that do so are bad. It is simply to say that a closer look should be given to what kinds of causes are doing so and why. Without such an examination, it will be possible to justify any policy, and any expansion of government intervention, with little democratic oversight. However, the consequences go far beyond even that considerable danger.

Militarization of the Environment

The first additional danger is the potential for the militarization of the environment. While many environmentalists have pushed the concept of environmental security on the basis that it will lead to a diversion of defense funding and technology and give greater priority to environmental policy, there is a likelihood that the strategy would backfire and lead instead to the military's co-opting environmental policy. Indeed, very little diversion has occurred, but much profoundly negative attention has been given to environmental issues.

The incursion of the military into environmental affairs is cause for great concern. As far back as 1991, some authors had outlined the risks of military involvement in environmental issues. Those risks include an institutional tendency toward secrecy and control of information, a propensity for conflictual thinking (i.e., the perception of "them vs. us"), and calls for mass mobilization against the perceived threat. Of great concern, too, is the potential for contravention of civil liberties as the military takes one more step into civilian affairs.

Conversely, there is a danger when civilian agencies make incursions into the military sphere, as the Environmental Protection Agency (EPA) for instance has done in its involvement in military activity in the Arctic, discussed below. The militarization of EPA policy is hardly a desirable objective. Unfortunately, it is already happening. As if to underscore the point, EPA recently published a brochure describing its role in environmental security; depicted on its cover were a group of fish, an eagle, a CH-53 helicopter, and a U.S. Navy destroyer all floating in harmony around a large tree.

The Tenuous Link Between Environment and War

It is an article of faith that the world faces imminent "water wars." Former United Nations secretary-general Boutros Boutros-Ghali once predicted that "the next war in the Middle East will be over water, not oil." But scrutiny of the historical record reveals that scarcities of renewable environmental resources have rarely been a direct cause of wars between states. There are arguably only two relevant cases in recent history. During the intermittent Anglo-Icelandic "Cod War" of the 1970s, a dispute over access to dwindling fish stocks, British and Icelandic vessels played chicken in the frigid waters off Iceland. The 100-hour Honduran-Salvadoran "Soccer War" of 1969 was a far more serious affair. Sparked by soccer match incidents, its root causes lay in overcrowding and severe deforestation that over the years had driven thousands of Salvadorans across the border to an unwelcoming Honduras.

Geoffrey D. Dabelko, *Wilson Quarterly*, August 1999.

To put the problem differently, would we really want to leave important aspects of national security policymaking to the EPA? Yet if its current activities in the name of national security are anything to go by, that might well occur. According to William Nitze, assistant administrator of the agency, environmental security is the "minimization of environmental trends or conditions *involving other countries* that could, over time, have significant negative impacts on important U.S. interests." It is not hard to envision, on the basis of that orientation, a time when the EPA is involved in making foreign policy too. As Nitze himself declares, "These [environmental] problems point to the need for EPA to play a large role in implementing the U.S. Government foreign policy agenda.". . .

Granting the EPA the status of executor of national security policy is one step toward militarization of its activities, particularly as it works closely with the Department of Defense (DOD), and sets a dangerous precedent. The involvement of DOD in civilian affairs, on the other hand, does not bode well for openness and civil liberties. . . .

The potential for militarization of the environment is only the first objection to linking environmental degradation with national security. The second objection . . . is that the linkage could actually lead to a decrease in security because some activities might cause resentment overseas or even lead to war. In addition, pursuit of environmental goals overseas without regard to their cost and potential returns is imprudent at best and encourages extortion on the part of foreign governments with domestic environmental problems.

The Distraction Scenario

If environmental security activities distract from the primary purpose of the military—defense—to the extent that the ability to accomplish the latter mission is compromised, then they become cause for serious concern. To be fair, such a situation is not yet in sight. Funding for environmental security programs at DOD, for example, is $3.9 billion for fiscal 2000, or 1.5 percent of the total defense budget. . . .

The Conflict Scenario

The more likely consequence of environmental security policies, however, is an increased propensity for conflict. One of the key elements of this trend has been the projection of domestic issues into the international arena. The case of the EPA illustrates the problem. Once an agency that dealt with purely internal affairs, EPA now carries out a variety of programs overseas. This is the inevitable consequence of a security policy that emphasizes tackling global ills. The *National Security Strategy* of 1998 epitomized the approach when it declared that "the dividing line between domestic and foreign policy is increasingly blurred." The implicit assumption underlying such a statement is that any country's problems are America's problems. That was made clear in Gore's statement in which he treated the global environment as a national security issue. Exactly where America's responsibilities stop and other countries' begin is a question left unanswered, as William Nitze at the EPA has demonstrated. In outlining his view of the tasks ahead, he declared that "the potential radioactive pollution of the Arctic . . . , climate change and ozone depletion are just the first three on what may become a long list of environmental threats to the U.S. that need to be addressed internationally." By the end of 1999 the *National Security Strategy* had added to that list, declaring that environmental threats to U.S. security also resulted from the introduction of nuisance plant and animal species; the over-harvesting of fish, forests, and other living natural resources; and the transnational movement of hazardous chemicals and waste. Where this list might end, and how long U.S. taxpayers will be prepared to foot the bill, is anyone's guess.

As America seeks to solve all the world's environmental problems, it should realize that some paths could lead to conflict. There are two ways in which this could happen, as we have already seen. The first is for the United States to prepare to get involved in other countries' disputes that are environmentally induced or include environmental factors. The second is efforts to cajole countries into abiding by certain standards, or actual intervention in the domestic affairs of other countries to sort out an environmental issue; such behavior could lead to resentment against the United States. Intervention may be welcomed initially by the country in question, particularly if intervention involves an influx of U.S. money, but welcome may quickly turn to resentment if projects come with too many strings attached, hurt economic growth, or deal with sensitive issues of national security. That could easily happen, as the case study of the Russian nuclear waste problem demonstrates.

Conceptions of environmental security are, therefore, just as much about conflict as they are about cooperation and peace, even under the well-being model of environmental security. The implication of these policies is that the goal of a sound environment is superior to that of maintaining peace. Indeed, that is the logic of most conceptions of environmental security, even when it is not always stated explicitly, or even realized, by those obsessed with solving the world's environmental problems. For the moment, some U.S. agencies are acting as if all environmental harm, anywhere in the world, requires strong American action and are forgetting the risks and moral issues involved. Yet peace is one of the most vital of national interests, and to override it in pursuit of other goals requires some compelling justification. It is ironic that pursuing a well-being approach to environmental security could lead the United States to the type of war that the planners for the conflict model wish to prevent. It is also highly ironic that war, which is probably the greatest cause of environmental destruction, could be the outcome of policies aimed at safeguarding the global environment.

The Extortion Scenario

By treating environmental problems around the globe as a national security issue, the United States also leaves itself open to subtle (and not so subtle) forms of blackmail and extortion. Any country with environmental problems can declare—either directly or by citing (or exaggerating) the potential for internal or regional strife as a result of the problem—that it needs urgent assistance from the United States because the problem constitutes a threat to U.S. national security. . . .

Foreign aid then will be portrayed to Congress and the American public as a matter of national security, not a humanitarian or developmental issue. Access to the American treasury then becomes far more likely. . . .

A Double Bind

The broad redefinition of security that is taking shape sets too many dangerous precedents, as the study of environmental security shows. International order will be severely destabilized if the United States becomes fixated on solving every problem that arises around the globe. The expansion of the concept of security also faces a double bind. If it results in militarization of policy previously restricted to the civilian sphere, as is happening in areas such as the environment and drug-trafficking control, the cost to society will be very high. If it instead leads to everything in the civilian sphere's being called an issue of national security, then the government will be able to bypass existing checks on its power by invoking "national security." At that point, anything is possible and abuses are probable.

It is important to proceed with greater caution and broader debate instead of blundering ahead regardless of the consequences. Addressing environmental issues is one thing; treating them as a threat to national security is quite another. By failing to differentiate reasonably between the two concepts, we may well find ourselves with more wars, more wasted money, and less security for all.

Periodical Bibliography

The following articles have been selected to supplement the diverse views presented in this chapter. Addresses are provided for periodicals not indexed in the *Readers' Guide to Periodical Literature*, the *Alternative Press Index*, the *Social Sciences Index*, or the *Index to Legal Periodicals and Books*.

Rebecca L. Adamson — "'Whole Earth' Economy," *Ms.*, September/October 1997.

Sharon Begley — "Butterflies Aren't Free," *Newsweek*, May 26, 1997.

Wendell Berry — "In Distrust of Movements," *Orion*, Summer 1999.

Lester Brown and Christopher Flavin — "A New Economy for a New Century," *Humanist*, May/June 1999.

Kenneth W. Chilton — "Economic Growth vs. the Environment," *Vital Speeches*, June 1, 1999.

Ken Conca — "The Environment-Security Trap," *Dissent*, Summer 1998.

Geoffrey D. Dabelko — "The Environmental Factor," *Wilson Quarterly*, August 1999.

James Dunn — "Can the Greens Destroy Nature?" *21st Century Science and Technology*, Winter 1998/1999.

David Ehrenfield — "The Ginkgo and the Stump," *Orion*, Autumn 1997.

Mark Hertsgaard — "A Green Foreign Policy," *Nation*, May 8, 2000

Marc A. Levy — "Exploring Environment-Security Connections," *Environment*, January/February 1999.

Roger E. Meiners and Bruce Yandle — "Get the Government Out of Environmental Control," *USA Today*, May 1996.

Jonathan Rowe — "Bad Company," *Dollars And Sense*, July/August 1998.

Sierra — "Has Environmentalism Become Too Extreme?" January/February 1998.

Alexander Volokh — "Shades of Green," *Reason*, May 1998.

Bruce Yandle — "Property Rights and Constitutional Order," *Vital Speeches*, June 15, 1998.

For Further Discussion

Chapter 1

1. Ronald Bailey argues that past predictions of environmental doom have not come true. Is this a valid response, in your view, to the predictions made by Eugene Linden? Explain.

2. What evidence do Ross Gelbspan and S. Fred Singer cite in their determinations over whether global warming has become a serious problem? Which do you find more persuasive? Why?

3. The American Council on Science and Health is largely funded by private corporations, including chemical manufacturers. Greenpeace is an organization that depends in part on raising public concern and fears about the environment in order to raise funds. Should either or both of these facts be considered in evaluating their respective arguments? Defend your answer.

Chapter 2

1. Kenneth W. Chilton says that setting standards so as to attain "zero risk" from air pollution is a mistaken goal. What argument does he use to support his assertion? Do you agree or disagree? Explain.

2. Do Allen Hershkowitz and Lynn Scarlett focus on economic costs and benefits of recycling, or do they include non-economic factors? In your opinion, should factors outside economics play a major part in the recycling debate? Why or why not?

3. After reading the articles of John Ritch and Arjun Makhijani, would you object to having a nuclear facility close to where you live? Explain.

Chapter 3

1. David Schaller argues that people in richer "consuming" nations have a greater environmental impact than those in developing countries, while Peter Huber asserts the opposite. Who do you believe is right? Explain.

2. Why does Kathrin Day Lassila refer to some animals and plants as "weedy" or "subsidized" species? Is "weedy" an emotionally loaded term? Why does she think of them as a problem? Does Jane S. Shaw adequately address the phenomenon of "weedy species," in your view? Explain your answer.

3. Evaluate your own standard of living in light of the articles in this chapter. Are there aspects of your lifestyle you may wish to change? Should individuals feel responsible for their effects on the environment? Why or why not?

Chapter 4

1. Carol Estes quotes ecologist Aldo Leopold in arguing that economics should not be the final arbiter of environmental policy. Is Leopold's assertion, in your view, compatible or incompatible with the arguments in favor of the free market made by Terry L. Anderson and Jane S. Shaw? Explain.

2. After reading the views of Terry L. Anderson and Jane S. Shaw as well as the arguments of Carol Estes, do you think turning over national parks to private owners would be a good idea? Explain why or why not.

3. What fundamental beliefs regarding humanity's relationship to the natural world are expressed in the arguments of Kirkpatrick Sale and Walter Truett Anderson? Which beliefs are closer to your own views?

4. How does William A. Nitze define "environmental security"? Is his conception of environmental security different from that presented by Paul Benjamin? How would you define environmental security?

5. What do you think Paul Benjamin was trying to accomplish by beginning his essay with dramatic scenarios of wars in the years 2015 and 2020? After reading his arguments do you believe his predictions of the future to be realistic? Why or why not?

Organizations to Contact

The editors have compiled the following list of organizations concerned with the issues debated in this book. The descriptions are derived from materials provided by the organizations. All have publications or information available for interested readers. The list was compiled on the date of publication of the present volume; the information provided here may change. Be aware that many organizations take several weeks or longer to respond to inquiries, so allow as much time as possible.

American Council on Science and Health
1995 Broadway, 2nd Fl., New York, NY 10023-5860
(212) 362-7044 • fax: (212) 362-4919
e-mail: acsh@acsh.org • website: www.acsh.org

ACSH is a consumer education consortium concerned with, among other topics, issues related to the environment and health. The council publishes *Priorities* magazine and position papers such as "Global Climate Change and Human Health" and "Public Health Concerns About Environmental Polychlorinated Biphenyls."

Cato Institute
1000 Massachusetts Ave. NW, Washington, DC 20001-5403
(202) 842-0200 • fax: (202) 842-3490
e-mail: cato@cato.org • website: www.cato.org

The Cato Institute is a libertarian public policy research foundation dedicated to limiting the role of government and protecting individual liberties. The institute publishes the quarterly magazine *Regulation*, the bimonthly *Cato Policy Report*, and numerous books, including *Through Green-Colored Glasses: Environmentalism Reconsidered* and *Climate of Fear: Why We Shouldn't Worry About Global Warming*.

Competitive Enterprise Institute (CEI)
1001 Connecticut Ave. NW, Suite 1250, Washington, DC 20036
(202) 331-1010 • fax: (202) 331-0640
e-mail: info@cei.org • website: www.cei.org

CEI encourages the use of the free market and private property rights to protect the environment. It advocates removing governmental regulatory barriers and establishing a system in which the private sector would be responsible for the environment. CEI's publications include the monthly newsletter *CEI Update* and the *Environmental Briefing Book*.

Defenders of Wildlife
1101 14th St. NW, #1400, Washington, DC 20005
(202) 682-9400
e-mail: info@defenders.org • website: www.defenders.org
Defenders of Wildlife is dedicated to the protection of all native wild animals and plants in their natural communities. The organization focuses on the accelerating rate of extinction of species and the associated loss of biodiversity, and habitat alteration and destruction. The organization publishes *Defenders* magazine.

Earth Island Institute
300 Broadway, Suite 28, San Francisco, CA 94133
(415) 788-3666 • fax: (415) 788-7324
website: www.earthisland.org
The Earth Island Institute sponsors a variety of educational and political activities to promote the preservation and restoration of the earth's natural environment. It publishes *Earth Island Journal*.

Environmental Defense Fund
257 Park Ave. South, New York, NY 10010
(212) 505-2100 • fax: (212) 505-0892
website: www.edf.org
The fund is a public interest organization of lawyers, scientists, and economists dedicated to the protection and improvement of environmental quality and public health. It publishes brochures, fact sheets, and the bimonthly *EDF Letter*.

Environment Canada
10 Wellington St., Hull, Quebec, CANADA, K1A 0H3
(819) 997-2800
website: www.ec.gc.ca
Environment Canada is a department of the Canadian government whose goal is to achieve sustainable development in Canada through environmental protection and conservation. It publishes reports and fact sheets on a variety of environmental issues.

Foundation for Research on Economics and the Environment (FREE)
945 Technology Blvd., Suite 101F, Bozeman, MT 59718
(406) 585-1776 • fax: (406) 585-3000
e-mail: free@mcn.net • website: www.free-eco.org
FREE is a research and education foundation committed to freedom, environmental quality, and economic progress. It works to reform environmental policy by using the principles of private prop-

erty rights, the free market, and the rule of law. FREE publishes the quarterly newsletter *FREE Perspectives on Economics and the Environment* and produces a biweekly syndicated op-ed column.

Greenpeace USA
1436 U St. NW, Washington, DC 20009
(800) 326-0959 • fax: (202) 462-4507
e-mail: info@wdc.greenpeace.org
website: www.greenpeaceusa.org

Greenpeace opposes nuclear energy and the use of toxic chemicals and supports wildlife preservation. It uses controversial direct-action techniques and strives for media coverage of its actions in an effort to educate the public. It publishes the quarterly magazine *Greenpeace* and the books *Coastline* and *The Greenpeace Book on Antarctica*.

The Heritage Foundation
214 Massachusetts Ave. NE, Washington, DC 20002
(800) 544-4843 • (202) 546-4400 • fax: (202) 544-2260
e-mail: pubs@heritage.org • website: www.heritage.org

The Heritage Foundation is a conservative think tank that supports the principles of free enterprise and limited government in environmental matters. Its many publications include the following position papers: "Can No One Stop the EPA?" and "How to Help the Environment Without Destroying Jobs."

National Audubon Society
700 Broadway, New York, NY 10003
(212) 979-3000 • fax: (212) 979-3188
e-mail: webmaster@list.audubon.org • website: www.audubon.org

The society seeks to conserve and restore natural ecosystems, focusing on birds and other wildlife for the benefit of humanity and the earth's biological diversity. It publishes *Audubon* magazine and the *WatchList*, which identifies North American bird species that are at risk of becoming endangered.

Natural Resources Defense Council (NRDC)
40 W. 20th St., New York, NY 10011
(212) 727-2700
e-mail: nrdcinfo@nrdc.org • website: www.nrdc.org

NRDC is an environmental group composed of lawyers and scientists who conduct research, work to educate the public, and lobby and litigate for environmental issues. The council publishes the quarterly *Amicus Journal* as well as books, pamphlets, brochures, and reports, many of which are available on its website.

Negative Population Growth, Inc. (NPG)

1608 20th St. NW, Suite 200, Washington, DC 20009
(202) 667-8950 • fax: (202) 667-8953
e-mail: npg@npg.org • website: www.npg.org

NPG works to educate the American public and political leaders about the detrimental effects of overpopulation on our environment and quality of life. NPG advocates a smaller, more sustainable U.S. population accomplished through voluntary incentives for smaller families and limits on immigration. NPG publishes position papers such as "Why We Need a Smaller U.S. Population and How We Can Achieve It" and "Immigration and U.S. Population Growth: An Environmental Perspective."

Political Economy Research Center (PERC)

502 S. 19th Ave., Suite 211, Bozeman, MT 59718-6872
(406) 587-9591 • fax: (406) 586-7555
e-mail: perc@perc.org • website: www.perc.org

PERC is a research and education foundation that focuses primarily on environmental and natural resource issues. It emphasizes the advantages of free markets and the importance of private property rights in environmental protection. PERC's publications include the monthly *PERC Reports* and papers in the PERC Policy Series such as "The Common Law: How It Protects the Environment."

Rainforest Action Network (RAN)

221 Pine St., Suite 500, San Francisco, CA 94104
(415) 398-4404 • fax: (415) 398-2732
e-mail: rainforest@ran.org • website: www.ran.org

RAN works to preserve the world's rain forests through activism addressing the logging and importation of tropical timber, cattle ranching in rain forests, and the rights of indigenous rainforest peoples. It also seeks to educate the public about the environmental effects of tropical hardwood logging. RAN's publications include the monthly *Action Report* and the semiannual *World Rainforest Report*.

Sierra Club

85 Second St., 2nd Fl., San Francisco, CA 94105-3441
(415) 977-5500 • fax: (415) 977-5799
e-mail: information@sierraclub.org • website: www.sierraclub.org

The Sierra Club is a nonprofit public interest organization that promotes conservation of the natural environment by influencing public policy decisions—legislative, administrative, legal, and electoral. It publishes *Sierra* magazine as well as books on the environment.

U.S. Environmental Protection Agency (EPA)
401 M St. SW, Washington, DC 20460
(202) 260-2090
website: www.epa.gov
The EPA is the government agency charged with protecting human health and safeguarding the natural environment. It works to protect Americans from environmental health risks, enforce federal environmental regulations, and ensure that environmental protection is an integral consideration in U.S. policy. The EPA publishes many reports, fact sheets, and educational materials.

U.S. Fish and Wildlife Service
1250 25th St. NW, Washington, DC 20037
(202) 293-4800
website: www.fws.gov
The U.S. Fish and Wildlife Service is a network of regional offices, national wildlife refuges, research and development centers, national fish hatcheries, and wildlife law-enforcement agents. The service's primary goal is to conserve, protect, and enhance fish and wildlife and their habitats. It publishes an endangered species list as well as fact sheets, pamphlets, and information on the Endangered Species Act.

Worldwatch Institute
1776 Massachusetts Ave. NW, Washington, DC 20036-1904
(202) 452-1999 • fax: (202) 296-7365
e-mail: worldwatch@worldwatch.org
website: www.worldwatch.org
Worldwatch is a research organization that analyzes and calls attention to global problems, including environmental concerns such as the loss of cropland, forests, habitat, species, and water supplies. It compiles the annual *State of the World* and *Vital Signs* anthologies and publishes the bimonthly *Worldwatch* magazine as well as position papers on environmental issues.

World Wildlife Fund (WWF)
1250 24th St., NW, PO Box 97180, Washington, DC 20077-7180
(800) 225-5993
website: www.worldwildlife.org
WWF works to save endangered species, to conduct wildlife research, and to improve the natural environment. It publishes an endangered species list, the bimonthly newsletter *Focus*, and a variety of books on the environment.

Bibliography of Books

Terry L. Anderson and Donald R. Leal — *Enviro-Capitalists: Doing Good While Doing Well.* Lanham, MD: Rowman and Littlefield, 1997.

Ronald Bailey, ed. — *Earth Report 2000: Revisiting the True State of the Planet.* New York: McGraw-Hill, 2000.

Wilfred Beckerman — *Through Green-Colored Glasses: Environmentalism Reconsidered.* Washington, DC: Cato Institute, 1996.

Sharon Beder — *Global Spin: The Corporate Assault on Environmentalism.* White River Junction, VT: Chelsea Green, 1998.

Lester Brown et al. — *State of the World 2000.* New York: W.W. Norton, 2000.

J. Baird Callicott and Michael P. Nelson, eds. — *The Great New Wilderness Debate.* Athens: University of Georgia Press, 1998.

Theo Colburn, Dianne Dumonoski, and John Peterson Myers — *Our Stolen Future: Are We Threatening Our Fertility, Intelligence, and Survival?: A Scientific Detective Story.* New York: Plume, 1997.

Ken Conca and Geoffrey D. Dabelko, eds. — *Green Planet Blues: Environmental Politics from Stockholm to Kyoto.* Boulder, CO: Westview, 1998.

Robert Costanza et al. — *An Introduction to Ecological Economics.* Boca Raton, FL: St. Lucie Press, 1997.

James A. Dunn Jr. — *Driving Forces: The Automobile, Its Enemies and the Politics of Mobility.* Brooking Institution Press, 1998.

Gregg Easterbrook — *A Moment on the Earth: The Coming Age of Environmental Optimism.* New York: Viking, 1995.

Paul R. Ehrlich and Anne H. Ehrlich — *Betrayal of Science and Reason: How Anti-Environmental Rhetoric Threatens Our Future.* Washington, DC: Island Press, 1996.

Evan Eisenberg — *The Ecology of Eden.* New York: Alfred A. Knopf, 1998.

Carl Frankel — *In Earth's Company: Business, Environment, and the Challenge of Sustainability.* Stony Creek, CT: New Society, 1998.

Michael Fumento — *Polluted Science: The EPA's Campaign to Expand Clean Air Regulations.* Washington, DC: AEI Press, 1997.

Ross Gelbspan	*The Heat Is On: The High Stakes Battle over Earth's Threatened Climate*. Reading, MA: Addison-Wesley, 1997.
Keven Graham and Gary Chandler	*Environmental Heroes: Success Stories of People at Work for the Earth*. Boulder, CO: Pruett, 1996.
Paul Hawken et al.	*Natural Capitalism: Creating the Next Industrial Revolution*. New York: Little, Brown, 1999.
Martha Honey	*Ecotourism and Sustainable Development: Who Owns Paradise?* Washington, DC: Island Press, 1999.
Peter Huber	*Hard Green: Saving the Environment from the Environmentalists: A Conservative Manifesto*. New York: Basic Books, 1999.
J. Robert Hunter	*Simple Things Won't Save the Earth*. Austin: University of Texas Press, 1997.
Jane Holtz Kay	*Asphault Nation: How the Automobile Took over America and How We Can Take It Back*. New York: Crown, 1997.
Thomas Gale Moore	*Climate of Fear: Why We Shouldn't Worry About Global Warming*. Washington, DC: Cato Institute, 1998.
S. George Philander	*Is the Temperature Rising? The Uncertain Science of Global Warming*. Princeton, NJ: Princeton University Press, 1998.
Philip Shabecoff	*Earth Rising: American Environmentalism in the 21st Century*. Washington, DC: Island Press, 2000.
Clifford J. Sherry	*Endangered Species: A Reference Handbook*. Santa Barbara, CA: ABC-CLIO, 1998.
Sandra Steingraber	*Living Downsteam: An Ecologist Looks at Cancer and the Environment*. New York: Addison-Wesley, 1997.
Brian Tokar	*Earth for Sale: Reclaiming Ecology in the Age of Corporate Greenwash*. Boston: South End Press, 1997.
Mathis Wackernagel and William E. Rees	*Our Ecological Footprint: Reducing Human Impact on the Earth*. Philadelphia: New Society Publishers, 1996.

Index